Grade
6

SPECTRUM®
Common Core
Language Arts and Math

Published by Spectrum®
An imprint of Carson-Dellosa Publishing LLC
Greensboro, North Carolina

Spectrum®
An imprint of Carson-Dellosa Publishing LLC
P.O. Box 35665
Greensboro, NC 27425 USA

ISBN 978-1-4838-0454-5

01-031141151

Table of Contents

Introduction to the Common Core State Standards
Grade 6

Why Are Common Core State Standards Important for My Child?
The Common Core State Standards are a set of guidelines that outline what children are expected to learn at school. Most U.S. states have voluntarily adopted the standards. Teachers, principals, and administrators in these states use the standards as a blueprint for classroom lessons, district curriculum, and statewide tests. The standards were developed by a state-led collaboration between the Council of Chief State School Officers (CCSSO) and the National Governors Association (NGA).

The Common Core Standards set high expectations for your child's learning. They are up-to-date with 21st century technology and draw on the best practices of excellent schools around the world. They focus on important skills in reading, language arts, and math. Common Core State Standards aim to ensure that your child will be college and career ready by the end of high school and able to compete in our global world.

What Are the Common Core State Standards for My Sixth Grade Student?
Common Core State Standards for your sixth grader are designed to strengthen reading and writing skills and deepen mathematical understanding. On practice pages in this book, you will find references to specific Common Core Standards that teachers will expect your child to know by the end of the year. Completing activities on these pages will help your child master essential skills for success in sixth grade.

A Sample of Common Core Language Arts Skills for Grade 6
- Provide a summary of a story or article that does not include personal opinions or judgments.
- Explain how an author uses point of view in a story.
- Use information presented in different ways (in charts, graphs, text, etc.).
- Think about the reasons an author gives to back up his or her points.
- Conduct research and write short research reports.
- Make sure pronouns agree with the nouns that precede them.
- Use commas, parentheses, and dashes to set off less important information in a sentence.
- Study Greek and Latin word roots.
- Learn about metaphors, personification, and other figures of speech.

A Sample of Common Core Math Skills for Grade 6
- Write ratios and proportions to show relationships between numbers.
- Work with percentages of whole numbers.
- Divide fractions by fractions.
- Add, subtract, multiply, and divide numbers with decimal points.
- Understand negative numbers.
- Write and solve simple algebraic equations.
- Find the area, surface area, and volume of shapes.
- Given a set of data, find the mean, median, and range.

© Copyright 2010. National Governors Association Center for Best Practices and Council of Chief State School Officers. All rights reserved.

How to Use This Book
In this book, you will find a complete **Common Core State Standards Overview** for sixth grade English Language Arts (pages 6–9) and Math (pages 64–67). Read these pages to learn more about the Common Core Standards and what you can expect your child to learn at school this year.

Then, choose **Practice Pages** that best address your child's needs for building skills that meet specific standards. Help your child complete practice pages and check the answers.

At the bottom of each practice page, you will find a **Helping at Home** tip that provides fun and creative ideas for additional practice with the skill at home.

Common Core State Standards for English Language Arts*

The following parent-friendly explanations of sixth grade Common Core English language arts standards are provided to help you understand what your child will learn in school this year. Practice pages listed will help your child master each skill.

Complete Common Core State Standards may be found here: www.corestandards.org.

RL/RI.6 Reading Standards for Literature and Informational Text

Key Ideas and Details
(Standards: RL.6.1, RL.6.2, RL.6.3, RI.6.1, RI.6.2, RI.6.3)

After reading, your child will find evidence in the text to answer questions and back up observations. He or she will use information that is directly stated and make inferences, or reasonable conclusions, about what is not directly stated.
• **Practice pages: 10–15, 20–22, 26, 27**

After reading, your child will decide on the main idea or theme of the text and explain how it is supported by details. He or she will summarize only what the text says without including personal opinion. • **Practice pages: 10–15, 18, 19, 21–24, 28, 29**

Your child will notice what changes during the course of a story or a nonfiction article. For example, your child will think about how characters respond to events in a story and change as a result or how a series of discoveries led to a scientific theory.
• **Practice pages: 10–15, 20, 21, 23, 24**

Craft and Structure
(Standards: RL.6.4, RL.6.5, RL.6.6, RI.6.4, RI.6.5, RI.6.6)

Your child will find unknown words and phrases in a text and use strategies (examples: searching for context clues, asking questions) to find their meanings. He or she will investigate words that create images, evoke emotions, or have specialized or technical meanings.
• **Practice pages: 12–15, 18, 19, 22, 25–29**

Your child will look closely at a particular sentence, paragraph, scene, chapter, stanza, or section and think about how it contributes to the overall meaning of the text.
• **Practice pages: 26, 27**

Your child will think about who is telling the story or explaining an idea. He or she will think about an author's purpose and consider how point of view affects the way a story is told.
• **Practice pages: 10, 11, 16, 17, 26, 27**

Integration of Knowledge and Skills
(Standards: RI.6.7, RI.6.8)

Your child will read and analyze information presented in a variety of formats: in text, charts, graphs, diagrams, time lines, etc. • **Practice pages: 28, 29**

Your child will think about the claims or arguments an author makes and decide if they are supported by valid reasons and evidence explained in the text. • **Practice pages: 22, 23**

W.6 Writing Standards

Text Types and Purposes
(Standards: W.6.1, W.6.2, W.6.3)

Your child will write arguments, supporting claims with sound reasons and trustworthy evidence. • **Practice pages: 30–33**

Your child will write to provide information in articles and research reports. He or she will organize information using strategies such as categorization, compare/contrast, and cause/effect. • **Practice pages: 34–37**

Your child will write real or fictional stories that include dialogue and well-developed characters, settings, and plots. • **Practice pages: 38–41**

Research to Build and Present Knowledge
(Standards: W.6.7, W.6.8)

Your child will conduct research projects to answer questions using several sources.
• **Practice page: 34**

Your child will gather information from a variety of print and digital sources and determine whether each is a reliable and trustworthy source of information. • **Practice page: 36**

Common Core State Standards for English Language Arts*

L.6 Language Standards

Conventions of Standard English
(Standards: L.6.1a, L.6.1b, L.6.1c, L.6.1d, L.6.1e, L.6.2a, L.6.2b)

Your child will practice using pronouns carefully and correctly in different parts of sentences. He or she will learn to check pronouns when proofreading and ask, "Does this pronoun take the place of a noun that came before it? Does it match the noun that it replaces?"
• **Practice pages: 42, 43, 45, 46**

Your child will learn to use intensive pronouns such as myself *and* ourselves. *These pronouns refer back to the subject in sentences like this:* We cleared the trail ourselves.
• **Practice page: 44**

Your child will consider the differences between informal and formal speaking and writing. He or she will think about ways to use Standard English, such as avoiding double negatives (example: She doesn't have any *instead of* She doesn't have none*).* • **Practice page: 47**

Your child will learn to use punctuation to set off less important information in sentences. He or she will use commas (example: Our teacher, Ms. Hall, is absent*), parentheses (example:* The party (for sixth graders only) is tonight*), or dashes (example:* The strawberries—my favorites—are ripe*) around non-essential information.* • **Practice pages: 48–50**

Your child will learn to check writing carefully for spelling. He or she will learn the spellings of words that are frequently confused (such as effect *and* affect*) or frequently misspelled (such as* column*).* • **Practice page: 51**

Knowledge of Language
(Standard: L.6.3a)

Your child will learn to mix up long and short sentences and sentences that begin in different ways in order to make his or her writing more lively and interesting. • **Practice page: 52**

Vocabulary Acquisition and Use
(Standards: L.6.4a, L.6.4b, L.6.4c, L.6.5a, L.6.5b, L.6.5c)

Your child will use context clues to figure out the meanings of unknown words. He or she will search the surrounding text for clues to the new word's meaning. • **Practice pages: 18, 19, 25**

Your child will study Greek and Latin word roots. He or she will learn that many words have roots that provide clues to their meaning. For example, since the root man *means "hand," the related word* manual *means "by hand."* • **Practice pages: 53–56**

Your child will learn the habit of looking up words in a dictionary or thesaurus to check their meanings, pronunciations, or parts of speech. • **Practice page: 57**

Your child will look for and understand examples of figurative language, or words that create images. Figurative language techniques include metaphors (example: The dancer was a floating petal) and personification (example: The sun smiled at me). • **Practice pages: 58, 59**

Your child will find relationships between words to study their meanings. He or she will solve analogies and other word puzzles by thinking about how words are alike or different and asking, "Do the words belong to the same category? Do they show cause and effect? Are they opposites?" • **Practice pages: 60, 61**

Your child will think about the differences between what words actually mean and what feelings they evoke. He or she will notice words that have positive connotations (such as relaxed) and negative connotations (such as lazy) and think about how to use them carefully in writing. • **Practice pages: 62, 63**

Making Inferences

Read the story. Answer the questions that follow.

It's Not My Fault

Almost every day, I eat lunch with Heather. Tracy is my friend, too, but she usually eats with Jordan. Every now and then, I eat lunch at their table, but not today. Tracy was angry at me. I needed Heather's advice.

"Tracy says I'm a liar," I said as I took a bite of my sandwich.

"About what?" Heather asked.

"It doesn't matter. I'm honest, right?"

"Honest about what?" Heather sipped her milk.

"Honest. You know, trustworthy, direct, truthful," I smiled.

Heather hesitated and then nodded. "Yeah, except the time you lied to your parents about your grades. And then the time you . . ."

"Grades don't count, and going shopping with Tracy doesn't count, either."

"Shopping with Tracy?" Heather looked confused.

"It's not my fault Tracy didn't want you to come. I didn't want to hurt your feelings. So, she told me to tell you I was sick."

"So you lied to me," Heather accused, raising her voice.

"I didn't lie. Tracy made up the lie."

"Don't blame Tracy because you lied to me," Heather said as she ripped the wrapping off her brownie.

"It's not my fault. You're way too sensitive," I said, gulping my milk.

"Maddie, the point is simple. You lie to your friends and then blame them for your mistakes. So, no, you're not really honest."

I could see that Heather was still hurt about Tracy. She didn't understand my problem. "I gotta go," I said. "See you tomorrow."

1. The story is told from the point of view of
   A. Heather.
   B. Maddie.
   C. Jordan.
   D. Tracy.

2. Which detail from the story is true?
   A. Heather and Tracy went shopping together.
   B. Heather needed Maddie's advice.
   C. Maddie always eats lunch with Tracy.
   D. Maddie usually eats lunch with Heather.

3. Maddie lied to Heather when she
   A. told Heather about a test grade.
   B. told Heather about her problems with Tracy.
   C. told Heather that she was sick.
   D. invited Heather to go shopping.

4. The title of the story is "It's Not My Fault" because
   A. Maddie thinks she is not at fault.
   B. Maddie is not at fault.
   C. Heather is confused.
   D. Tracy is angry.

5. When Maddie says, "Grades don't count," the reader knows that
   A. Maddie doesn't care about grades.
   B. Maddie is an honest person.
   C. Maddie doesn't understand that a lie is a lie.
   D. Maddie always gets good grades.

6. At the end of the story, the character with the best understanding about the problem of lying is
   A. Maddie.
   B. Jordan.
   C. Heather.
   D. Tracy.

7. The theme of this story is
   A. a friend doesn't care if you tell an occasional lie.
   B. no matter how you explain it, lying is lying.
   C. some lies don't count.
   D. it's OK to lie to keep from hurting someone's feelings.

Helping at Home

Ask your child to think about what each character might do and say at lunchtime the next day. Who will Maddie sit with? What will she and her friends talk about? Your child may wish to continue the story and write the next event.

Making Inferences

Read the story. Answer the questions that follow.

Standing Up

Kerry rode into shore, hopped off her board, and jogged over to where her cousins were sitting. "Are you two ready to give it a try?" she asked.

Miles took a deep breath and nodded. He was worried about looking silly, but he had a feeling he was going to love doing this. He expected it to feel like flying though the water or riding his bike down a steep hill without using the brakes.

Sophie looked up at Kerry with an eager expression. She loved to try new things and was usually good at them. She learned quickly and wasn't afraid to plunge in. Miles admired these characteristics, but knew he just wasn't as adventurous as his sister.

"OK," Kerry began, "let's start on long boards because they catch waves easily, giving beginners more time to stand. Just remember, never paddle out farther than you can swim back in. Pay attention to the weather. And always respect the ocean."

Kerry showed how to stand in the center of the board, between the nose and the tail. "Try to remember where the sweet spot is on your board," she explained. "When a wave catches the tail, start paddling."

"I had no idea this was so technical," Sophie said. "I'm ready to jump on and ride."

"Whoa, there," said Kerry. "Why don't we start by standing up a few times on the sand, where the board is stable? Then, we can head for the water. Who wants to go first?"

"Me," said Miles, standing up. "I'm ready to try."

1. Miles and Sophie are Kerry's
   A. friends
   B. cousins
   C. students
   D. siblings

2. Miles and Sophie are learning to
   A. swim
   B. sail
   C. surf
   D. float

3. Why does Miles think he is not as adventurous as his sister?
   A. because he is too afraid to try surfing
   B. because he thinks surfing will be too technical
   C. because he can't find the sweet spot
   D. because he feels nervous

4. What are the surfing terms for the front and back ends of a surfboard?
   A. *nose* and *tail*
   B. *head* and *foot*
   C. *up* and *down*
   D. *forward* and *aft*

5. Which is an unbiased summary of the story?
   A. Surfing is a lot of fun.
   B. Surfing is a difficult and dangerous sport.
   C. For beginners, surfing can be challenging but rewarding.
   D. Surfing is easy and fun.

6. Which is a simile?
   A. long board
   B. sweet spot
   C. plunge in
   D. like flying though the water

7. Why is the story titled "Standing Up"?
   A. because Miles will try to stand up and surf, even though he is nervous
   B. because Sophie already knows how to stand on a surfboard
   C. because Miles and Sophie are sitting on the beach
   D. because waves can knock you off a surfboard

Helping at Home

Talk about what it means to make inferences. It can also be described as *reading between the lines or drawing conclusions.* Describe a sport or activity without naming it. Can your child guess what you are talking about? Take turns.

Making Inferences

Read the story. Answer the questions that follow.

Shanda

When Shanda first arrived at her new school, she discovered to her dismay that a freckle-faced boy in her sixth-grade class was smitten with her. He didn't offer his name, just a handful of pretty flowers picked from outside.

Shanda soon learned the boy's name, Tommy. Whenever the class lined up for assembly or gym, he always smiled crookedly at her. Shanda did not like the attention. Why did he like her anyway? On several occasions, Shanda tried to start a conversation with Tommy. But he just blushed, put his hands in his pocket, and looked down in embarrassment.

Gradually, Shanda made friends and felt happy at her new school. The only thing that still made her uncomfortable was Tommy with his crooked, shy smiles.

One day in the hallway, Tommy came up to her. "Do you like animals?" he asked shyly. Shanda was shocked that Tommy had spoken to her.

"Hi, Tommy," she said. "Yes, I love animals. How about you?"

Tommy looked very nervous. He whispered something about a dog and then hurried away. Shanda wondered if she had hurt his feelings by calling him Tommy. Maybe he liked to be called Tom.

A week later, Tommy reverently handed Shanda a photo of a beautiful collie. She had sleek fur and intelligent eyes. Her ears were alert, and her face tilted as if she were asking a question. Shanda could tell that this dog was important to Tommy. "What's her name?" she asked softly.

"Sh-, sh-, she was Shanda...like you. We had her since I was in kindergarten. Sh-, she's gone now."

1. From whose point of view is this story told?
   A. Tommy's
   B. the teacher's
   C. Shanda's
   D. Shanda's friend

2. Which word best describes Shanda's attitude toward Tommy at the beginning of the story?
   A. smitten
   B. annoyed
   C. angry
   D. hopeful

3. Which word best describes Shanda's attitude toward Tommy at the end of the story?
   A. annoyed
   B. sad
   C. dismissive
   D. sympathetic

4. We can conclude that
   A. Tommy's dog died, and he misses her.
   B. Tommy's family now has a cat.
   C. Tommy likes the name Shanda.
   D. Tommy wants Shanda to be his girlfriend.

5. What probably caused Tommy to give Shanda flowers?
   A. He felt sorry for her because she was new.
   B. She and his dog shared a name.
   C. She had the same hair color as his collie.
   D. She was an animal lover like him.

6. In this story, what does *smitten* mean?
   A. struck by
   B. attacked by
   C. attracted to
   D. bothered by

7. Which is an unbiased summary of the story?
   A. A terribly shy boy makes a friend.
   B. A new girl is unfriendly to a shy boy.
   C. A boy's love for his dog helps him make a new friend.
   D. Moving to a new school is the worst.

Helping at Home Ask your child to think about how the story would be different if it were told from Tommy's point of view. Together, brainstorm a good first sentence for the new story. Encourage your child to write it down and continue the new story.

Point of View

When a writer writes a story, he or she chooses a narrator to tell the story. In some stories, the narrator is one of the characters in the story. Words such as *I, me,* and *my* let readers know that this is happening. This is called **first-person point of view**. Here is an example from the science fiction story "The Colony."

As I followed the track, I realized that I was tight all over. My toes, fingers, and even my teeth were clenched. I jogged a few steps and shook my arms out. In training, they had always told you to stay relaxed. If you were tense, you couldn't respond as quickly. *Respond to what?* I thought. *Who in the world could be out here?*

I suppose the jogging and unclenching distracted me. It wasn't until I was fully at the top of the hill that I saw the crater and what was in it. I automatically held my Telewave up to my mouth.

"Jasper Colony, this is Morgan. Get me the Chairman," I said. A crackle assured me that my call was being transmitted. Then, the abrupt bark of the Chairman's voice made me jump.

"Morgan, what are you doing out there?" the Chairman asked.

Here is the same scene, but it is written in **third-person point of view**. Readers see words such as *he, she, him, her, his, they,* and *them* in stories that are written in third person. The narrator is not a character in the story. The main character is the same, but the **omniscient**, or all-knowing, narrator "reports" to readers what the character says, thinks, and does.

As he followed the track, Morgan realized that he was tight all over. His toes, fingers, and even his teeth were clenched. He jogged a few steps and shook his arms out. In training, they had always told him to stay relaxed. If he were tense, he couldn't respond as quickly. *Respond to what?* he thought. *Who in the world could be out here?*

He supposed the jogging and the unclenching distracted him. It wasn't until he was fully at the top of the hill that he saw the crater and what was in it. He automatically held his Telewave up to his mouth.

"Jasper Colony, this is Morgan. Get me the Chairman," he said. A crackle assured him that his call was being transmitted. Then, the abrupt bark of the Chairman's voice made him jump.

"Morgan, what are you doing out there?" the Chairman asked. He felt that things were beginning to get out of hand.

Point of View

Look back at the story part on page 16. What do you think is in the crater? What happens next? Write the next paragraph in first-person point of view. Remember, in first person the narrator is a character in the story. Readers learn what he or she is thinking and feeling. The narrator does not know what other characters are thinking and feeling.

_____

_____

_____

_____

_____

_____

_____

_____

_____

Now, write that same scene in third-person point of view. Remember, Morgan is still the main character. The all-knowing narrator is not a character, but will tell what Morgan says, thinks, and does. The narrator will also tell what any other character says, thinks, and does.

_____

_____

_____

_____

_____

_____

_____

_____

_____

Helping at Home

Read the story versions your child wrote on this page and talk about the effect that point of view has on you as a reader. How does it change the way you think about the story and characters? Do you prefer one version? How about your child?

Word Choice

Read the poem and answer the questions that follow.

The Ant and the Cricket

A silly young cricket, who decided to sing
Through the warm sunny months of summer and spring,
Began to complain when he found that at home
His cupboards were empty and winter had come.

At last by starvation the cricket made bold
To hop through the wintertime snow and the cold.
Away he set off to a miserly ant
To see if to keep him alive he would grant
Shelter from rain, a mouthful of grain.
"I wish only to borrow—I'll repay it tomorrow—
If not, I must die of starvation and sorrow!"

Said the ant to the cricket, "It's true I'm your friend,
But we ants never borrow, we ants never lend;
We ants store up crumbs so when winter arrives
We have just enough food to keep ants alive."

1. What is the definition of *cupboards* in the poem?
   ☐ where books are stored   ☑ where food is stored   ☐ where shoes are stored

2. What is the definition of *miserly* in the poem?
   ☑ selfish/stingy   ☐ generous/kind   ☐ mean/ugly

3. What is the definition of *grant* in the poem?
   ☐ to take away   ☐ to belch   ☐ to give

4. In two sentences, describe what the poet is trying to say.

   _____

   _____

   _____

Encourage your child to share with you when he or she learns a new word such as *miserly*. Make a game of trying to use the new word in conversation with your child three times in one evening. If your child can't think of a word, suggest one.

Word Choice

Personification is a figure of speech in which human characteristics are given to an animal or object.

Example: The trees danced in the wind.

Trees do not dance; therefore, the trees are being personified.

Read the poem and answer the questions that follow.

The Eagle

1 He clasps the crag with crooked hands:
2 Close to the sun in lonely lands,
3 Ringed with the azure world, he stands.

4 The wrinkled sea beneath him crawls;
5 He watches from his mountain walls,
6 And like a thunderbolt he falls.

—Alfred, Lord Tennyson

1. What is the correct definition of *crag*?_____

_____

2. What is the correct definition of *azure*? _____

_____

3. Which phrases in the poem show personification?_____

_____

4. Explain what one of these phrases actually means. _____

_____

_____

5. What is the author trying to say in the last line of the poem?_____

_____

_____

Helping at Home

Encourage your child to search for and read the poem "The Tyger" by William Blake. Can he or she find examples in that poem of personification and other vivid language? What other animals would make good subjects for poems? Why?

19

Making Inferences

Read the text and answer the questions that follow.

Sydney, Australia

- Sydney is the capital of New South Wales, Australia.
- Manufacturing is a strong industry in Sydney. The city is also the headquarters of many large companies.
- Sydney is the major port of southeastern Australia.
- Sydney is Australia's largest city.
- The discovery of gold in 1851 increased Sydney's population. The population today is over 3 million people.
- Interesting sites in Sydney include the Sydney Opera House, the Sydney Harbour Bridge, and the Australia Square Tower, which is the country's largest skyscraper.

1. Why do you think large companies might choose to have their headquarters in Sydney?

   _____

   _____

   _____

2. Gold was discovered in Australia in what year?_____

3. Explain how the discovery of gold increased Sydney's population._____

   _____

   _____

4. Would you like to visit Sydney? Why or why not?_____

   _____

   _____

   _____

Ask your child if the answer for question #2 can be found in the text. (Yes.) Is the answer for #1 found in the text? (No.) Talk about the differences between the questions and how to answer them. Ask similar questions about the place where you live.

Helping at Home

Making Inferences

Read the text and answer the questions that follow.

Cairo, Egypt

- Cairo is the capital of Egypt.
- Cairo is the largest city of not only Egypt, but all of Africa and the Middle East.
- The population of Cairo is almost 7 million people.
- Cairo is the cultural center for the Islamic religion.
- Cairo is a major industrial site for Egypt.
- Cairo is a port on the Nile River near the head of the Nile delta.
- Interesting sites include the Egyptian Museum, the Sphinx, the pyramids, and the City of the Dead.

1. Many major cities, including Cairo, have a port. Why do you think large cities often develop near water?

   _____

   _____

   _____

2. Circle the statement that is an unbiased summary of the text.
   Cairo is an overcrowded city in Egypt.
   Everyone in Cairo, Egypt, likes to live near rivers.
   The large city of Cairo, Egypt, is a cultural and industrial center.

3. Would you like to visit Cairo? Why or why not?_____

   _____

   _____

   _____

   _____

Helping at Home

Based on the text about Cairo, Egypt, how many facts can you and your child state? How many opinions can you state? How many of your opinions can be backed up by facts from the text? Do a similar exercise about the place where you live.

Finding Supporting Evidence

Read the text and answer the questions that follow.

Jupiter

The planet Jupiter is the largest planet of our solar system and is named for the king of the gods. Its distinguishing feature is the Great Red Spot, which changes occasionally in both color and brightness. Jupiter has a thin ring and at least 16 moons. Jupiter is the first of the outer planets, separated from the inner planets by an asteroid belt. It is almost 500 million miles from the Sun and takes nearly 12 years to complete a revolution around the Sun. It rotates on its axis in approximately 10 hours. Jupiter does not have a solid surface but rather a surface of gaseous clouds.

1. Define the following words.

   *asteroid:*_____

   *gaseous:*_____

2. Approximately how far is Jupiter from the Sun?

   _____

3. What evidence from the text supports this opinion: Walking on Jupiter would be awful!

   _____

   _____

4. Write a three-sentence summary about Jupiter.

   _____

   _____

   _____

5. Why do you think ancient astronomers chose to name Jupiter after the king of the gods?

   _____

Helping at Home

Which fact about Jupiter does your child find most interesting? Is it the planet's size, number of moons, or distance from the Sun? Encourage your child to research that same fact for the other planets in our solar system and make a chart.

Main Ideas and Supporting Details

Read each passage and circle the main idea that it supports.

1. Not surprisingly, Tyrannosaurus had huge teeth in its mammoth head. They were 6 inches long! Because it was a meat eater, Tyrannosaurus's teeth were sharp. They looked like spikes! In comparison, the long-necked, plant-eating Mamenchisaurus had a tiny head and small, flat teeth.

    A. Scientists can't figure out why some dinosaurs had huge teeth.
    B. Tyrannosaurus was probably scarier looking than Mamenchisaurus.
    C. Meat-eating and plant-eating dinosaurs had specialized teeth.

2. Dinosaurs' names often reflect their size or some other physical trait. For example, *Compsognathus* means "pretty jaw." *Saltopus* means "leaping foot." *Lesothosaurus* means "lizard from Lesotho."

    A. Of the three species, Lesothosaurus was probably the fastest.
    B. Of the three species, Compsognathus was probably the fastest.
    C. Of the three species, Saltopus was probably the fastest.

3. Edmontosaurus, a huge three-ton dinosaur, had 1,000 teeth! The teeth were cemented into chewing pads in the back of Edmontosaurus's mouth. Unlike the sharp teeth of the meat-eating Tyrannosaurus, this dinosaur's teeth were flat.

    A. Edmontosaurus did not eat meat.
    B. Edmontosaurus did not eat plants.
    C. Edmontosaurus moved very fast.

Helping at Home

Watch a news, science, or information program on TV with your child. Can you each list three facts from the show? Can you each provide a summary that is based on those facts instead of on your own opinions?

Examples and Events

Read the text and answer the questions that follow.

Benjamin Franklin

Many great colonists made an impact on American history. Among them was Benjamin Franklin, who left his mark as a printer, author, inventor, scientist, and statesman. He has been called "the wisest American."

Franklin was born in Boston in 1706, one of 13 children in a very religious Puritan household. Although he had less than two years of formal education, his tremendous appetite for books served him well. At age 12, he became an apprentice printer at *The New England Courant* and soon began writing articles that poked fun at Boston society.

In 1723, Franklin ran away to Philadelphia, where he started his own newspaper. He was very active in the Philadelphia community. He operated a bookstore and was named postmaster. He also helped to establish a library, a fire company, a college, an insurance company, and a hospital. His well-known *Poor Richard's Almanac* was first printed in 1732.

Over the years, Franklin maintained an interest in science and mechanics, leading to such inventions as a fireplace stove and bifocal lenses. In 1752, he gained world fame with his kite-and-key experiment, which proved that lightning was a form of electricity.

Franklin was an active supporter of the colonies throughout the Revolutionary War. He helped to write and was a signer of the Declaration of Independence in 1776. In his later years, he skillfully represented America in Europe, helping to work out a peace treaty with Great Britain.

1. The main idea is:

   ☐ Many great colonists made an impact on American history.

   ☐ Benjamin Franklin was a great colonist who left his mark as a printer, author, inventor, scientist, and statesman.

2. How did Benjamin Franklin gain world fame? _____

3. What did Franklin sign and help to write? _____

4. Number in order the following accomplishments of Benjamin Franklin.

   _____ Served as representative of America in Europe
   _____ Began printing *Poor Richard's Almanac*
   _____ Experimented with electricity
   _____ Started his own newspaper
   _____ Helped to write and sign the Declaration of Independence
   _____ Served as apprentice printer on *The New England Courant*

Helping at Home

Encourage your child to keep a notebook of interesting people, events, and ideas. It might include astronaut Sally Ride, the sinking of the *Titanic*, or bird migration. Details about each topic can be added over time.

Words From Text

Read the text and answer the questions that follow.

Weather and Climate

The behavior of the atmosphere, which we experience as weather and climate, affects our lives in many important ways. It is the reason no one lives on the South Pole. It controls when a farmer plants the food we will eat, which crops will be planted, and also whether those crops will grow. The weather tells you what clothes to wear and how you will play after school. Weather is the sum of all the conditions of the air that may affect the Earth's surface and its living things. These conditions include the temperature, air pressure, wind, and moisture. Climate refers to these conditions but generally applies to larger areas and longer periods of time, such as the annual climate of South America rather than today's weather in Oklahoma City.

Climate is influenced by many factors. It depends first and foremost on latitude. Areas nearest the equator are warm and wet, while the poles are cold and relatively dry. The poles also have extreme seasonal changes, while the areas at the middle latitudes have more moderate climates, neither as cold as the poles nor as hot as the equator. Other circumstances may alter this pattern, however. Land near the oceans, for instance, is generally warmer than inland areas.

Elevation also plays a role in climate. For example, despite the fact that Africa's highest mountain, Kilimanjaro, is just south of the equator, its summit is perpetually covered by snow. In general, high land is cooler and wetter than nearby low land.

1. What is the correct definition for *atmosphere*?

☐ the clouds   ☐ the sky   ☐ where weather occurs

2. What is the correct definition for *foremost*?

☐ most important   ☐ highest number   ☐ in the front

3. What is the correct definition for *circumstances*?

☐ temperatures   ☐ seasons   ☐ conditions

4. What is the correct definition for *elevation*?

☐ height above Earth   ☐ nearness to equator   ☐ snow covering

5. What is the correct definition for *perpetually*?

☐ occasionally   ☐ rarely   ☐ always

Helping at Home

Before helping your child define a word, encourage him or her to use these strategies: use context clues to find the meaning; determine the meaning of root words, prefixes, or suffixes; think of related words; look up the word in a dictionary.

Author's Purpose

Read the text and answer the questions that follow.

Written in 1814 by Francis Scott Key, our American national anthem is stirring, beautiful, and difficult to sing. Key wrote the song while aboard a ship off the coast of Maryland, where one long night he watched the gunfire from a British attack on America's Fort McHenry. The following morning, he wrote "The Star-Spangled Banner" when, to his great joy, he saw the American flag still flying over the fort—a sign that the Americans had not lost the battle.

The Star-Spangled Banner

Oh say, can you see, by the dawn's early light,
What so proudly we hail'd at the twilight's last gleaming?
Whose broad stripes and bright stars, thro' the perilous fight,
O'er the ramparts we watch'd were so gallantly streaming?
And the rockets' red glare, the bombs bursting in air,
Gave proof thro' the night that our flag was still there.
Oh say, does that star-spangled banner yet wave
O'er the land of the free and the home of the brave?

Oh, the shore dimly seen thro' the mists of the deep,
Where the foe's haughty host in dread silence reposes,
What is that which the breeze, o'er the towering steep,
As it fitfully blows, half conceals, half discloses?
Now it catches the gleam of the morning's first beam,
In full glory reflected, now shines on the stream:
'Tis the star-spangled banner: O, long may it wave
O'er the land of the free and the home of the brave!

1. Who wrote "The Star-Spangled Banner"? _____

2. What is "The Star-Spangled Banner"? _____

3. In what year was the song written?_____

4. At what time of day was the song written? _____

5. Tell what is meant by the lines " . . . the rockets' red glare, the bombs bursting in air/Gave proof through the night that our flag was still there."

   _____

   _____

6. What is the correct definition of *ramparts?* _____

_____

7. What is the correct definition of *gallantly?* _____

_____

8. What is the correct definition of *haughty?* _____

_____

9. What is the correct definition of *reposes?* _____

_____

10. What was the author's purpose for writing "The Star-Spangled Banner"?
    A. to describe a battle
    B. to praise the beauty of his country
    C. to convince the enemy to give up
    D. to express pride in the strength of his country

11. The song is written from the point of view of
    A. a patriot
    B. a soldier
    C. a prisoner
    D. a politician

12. What feelings are evoked by the phrase *the mists of the deep?*

_____

_____

_____

Ask your child to share a favorite song. Challenge him or her to think about the lyrics and determine the author's purpose in writing the song. What specific words from the song show the writer's feelings and point of view?

Comparing Texts

Read the text and answer the questions that follow.

The Land Down Under

Australia and New Zealand are often referred to as the "land down under." The name, made popular by American soldiers stationed there during World War II, grew out of the idea that these two countries are opposite or below Europe on the globe. While Australia and New Zealand are often linked, they are individual countries, separated by more than 1,000 miles of ocean.

Their landscapes are quite different. New Zealand is made up of two main islands, North and South Island, which are nearly covered by snowy mountains. One of the most unusual and beautiful areas of New Zealand is the volcanic region around Lake Taupo on North Island. There you will see boiling springs, pools of steaming mud, hot-water geysers, small lakes with beds of brightly colored rocks, and waterfalls. While most of the people of New Zealand live and work in the industrialized cities, dairy farming is most important to the country's economy. The New Zealanders eat more meat and butter than people anywhere else in the world, and they sell huge amounts to other countries.

As in Australia, many of the customs in New Zealand would be familiar to a traveler from America because the two countries were settled by British settlers hundreds of years ago. However, the native islanders have descended from Asian ancestors, so the remnants of ancient Eastern practices exist alongside the European way of life.

1. The main idea is:

    ☐ Australia and New Zealand are often referred to as the "land down under."

    ☐ While Australia and New Zealand are often linked, they are individual countries.

2. What is the correct definition for *landscape*?

    ☐ natural scenery and features   ☐ mountainsides   ☐ natural resources

3. What is the correct definition for *economy*?

    ☐ thrifty   ☐ money management   ☐ countryside

4. What is the nickname for Australia and New Zealand?_____

5. What business is most important to the New Zealand economy?_____

6. Australia and New Zealand have similarities and differences. Complete the Venn diagram.

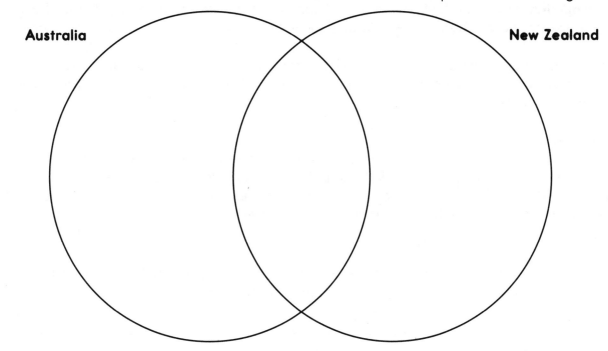

Australia   **New Zealand**

7. Using what you know about the United States and Australia, complete the Venn diagram.

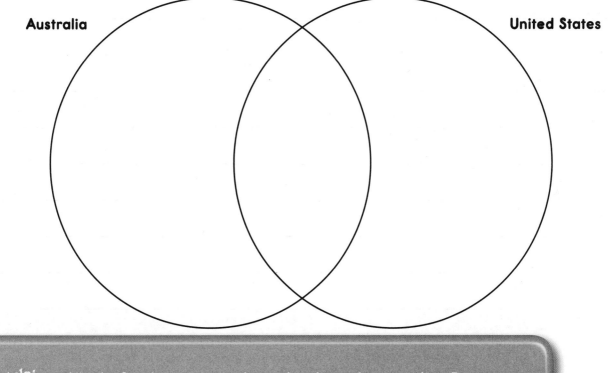

Australia   **United States**

Think of a place very similar to the place where you live. Discuss similarities and differences between the two places. Repeat the exercise with a place that is very different from your area. What could you read to learn more about the places?

Writing an Opinion

Your **opinion** is how you feel or think about something. Although other people may have the same opinion, their reasons could not be exactly the same because of their individuality.

When writing an opinion paragraph, it is important to first state your opinion. Then, in at least three sentences, support your opinion. Finally, end your paragraph by restating your opinion in different words.

Example:

    I believe dogs are excellent pets. For thousands of years, dogs have guarded and protected their owners. Dogs are faithful and have been known to save the lives of those they love. Dogs offer unconditional love as well as company for the quiet times in our lives. For these reasons, I feel that dogs make wonderful pets.

Write an opinion paragraph on whether you would or would not like to have lived in Colonial America. Be sure to support your opinion with at least three reasons.

_____

_____

_____

_____

_____

_____

_____

_____

_____

_____

Helping
at Home

Help your child access an online newspaper and choose an editorial to read about a social or political issue. Can your child locate the text where the author states his or her opinion? Can he or she find three reasons the author gives for the opinion?

Topics for Persuasive Writing

How do writers get readers to think, feel, or act in a certain way when they write persuasively? Often, they appeal to readers' emotions. When writers make an emotional appeal, they try to get at something about which readers feel strongly. For example, Ms. Martinez, a home economics teacher, thinks cooking classes are important. She included this statement in a letter to the editor:

> Our job is to prepare students for life beyond school. Computers and computer classes are available to students in many ways. Cooking classes, however, are available to students only while they are in middle school. If we don't offer cooking classes, we are not doing our jobs.
>
> Ms. Martinez

Ms. Martinez knows that most people feel strongly about doing their jobs well. She also knows that many people feel strongly about education and about their local schools. Though the statements are opinions (rather than facts), they have a strong emotional appeal and may persuade some readers to believe as the writer does.

Many people have strong feelings about positive issues such as these:

| justice | family | security | education |
| money | home | safety | conservation |

People may also have strong feelings toward negative issues such as these:

| injustice | crime | waste |
| violence | pollution | danger |

Name some issues about which you have strong feelings. State your opinion about each.

_____   _____

_____   _____

_____   _____

_____   _____

_____   _____

_____   _____

Helping at Home

Brainstorm topics that evoke strong feelings or differences of opinion among students in your child's class. They might include lunch menus or school parties. Ask your child to choose a topic and state an opinion with three supporting reasons.

Reasons, Facts, and Examples

To **persuade** means to convince someone that your opinion is correct. "Because I said so," isn't a very convincing reason. Instead, you need to offer reasons, facts, and examples to support your opinion.

Write two reasons or facts and two examples to persuade someone.

1. Riding a bicycle "no-handed" on a busy street is a bad idea.

    Reasons/Facts:_____

    _____

    Examples:_____

    _____

    _____

2. Taking medicine prescribed by a doctor for someone else is dangerous.

    Reasons/Facts:_____

    _____

    Examples:_____

    _____

    _____

3. Learning to read well will help you in every other subject in school.

    Reasons/Facts:_____

    _____

    Examples:_____

    _____

    _____

Helping at Home

Talk about what it means to be a *devil's advocate* and argue for a position you don't actually support. State an opinion that you know your child agrees with. Challenge him or her to argue against it using reasons, facts, and examples.

Organizing Reasons and Evidence

What class do you think your school should add to its course offerings? Decide on a new class, then write a letter to your teacher or principal. Try to persuade the person that your idea is a good one. Ask yourself this: What will make this person want to support my idea?

Before you begin drafting your letter, write your reasons here. Then, number them in the order in which you will use them in your letter. Save the strongest argument, or the most important reason, for last.

Reason: _____

Reason: _____

Reason: _____

Reason: _____

Dear _____,

_____

_____

_____

_____

_____

_____

_____

_____

_____

_____

© Carson-Dellosa • CD-704506

Read your child's letter, marking any errors you find and offering suggestions for revision. Encourage your child to write a clean copy of the letter and submit it to a teacher, the principal, or a school newspaper.

Choosing a Topic for Research

Writing a report is a good way to show what you know. It is also a good way to learn about a topic that interests you.

Choose topic and fill in the chart below.

Topic:_____

What I Know	What I Want to Know	How or Where I Might Find Out Information

Now, conduct some research and take notes. Remember to organize your notes by specific topic.

Helping at Home

Finding a topic that is not too broad or too narrow can be a challenge. Choose a broad topic such as *the ocean*. Ask your child to think of more focused topics that relate to the ocean. Talk about which would make good topics for a research report.

Cause and Effect

Why are school buses yellow? Why is cheese orange? When you ask why, you are looking for causes. A **cause** is a reason why something happens. An **effect** is a thing that happens. Here are some examples of causes and effects. Think about the relationship between each cause and effect.

Cause	Effect
It is raining.	Track practice is held indoors.
The lawn mower is broken.	The grass is knee high.
Tamara broke a tooth.	She went to the dentist today.

When writers write to explain, they often use causes and effects. They use the words and phrases *so*, *because*, *as a result*, and *therefore* to link causes and effects. Read this paragraph about why earthquakes occur. Circle the cause-and-effect words and phrases in the paragraph.

> The surface of Earth consists of huge geologic plates. On these plates rest the oceans and continents. The place where two plates meet is called a *fault*. Sometimes, one plate or the other shifts, so they rub against each other at the fault line. If there is enough shifting, something has to give. Both plates may buckle, or one plate may slip up over the edge of the other. Whatever the type of movement, if it is significant, the surface of Earth shakes or heaves as a result.

Can you find some causes and effects in the paragraph? One is written for you. Write two other causes and effects.

Cause	Effect
Earth's plates shift.	The plates rub against each other.

Helping at Home

Cause and effect is just one way to organize information. Think of a topic such as *Foods Around the World*. Challenge your child to think of ways to organize information about it: spatially, compare and contrast, by categories, etc.

Reliable Sources

Once you find a source that seems to have the information you need, you must decide whether the source is **reliable**. If the source is printed, ask yourself the following questions.

- **When was this source published?** If you need current information, the source should be only one or two years old.

- **Who wrote this source and for what purpose?** If the source is an encyclopedia, atlas, or almanac, you can be pretty confident that responsible authors wrote it to provide information. If it is a magazine article or a work of nonfiction, you need to ask more questions. Might there be bias in the material? Read the book jacket or an "About the Author" blurb to discover as much as you can about the expertise of the author and the purpose for writing.

If you are looking at an online source, there are some other questions to ask. Keep in mind that anyone can create a Web site. Just because you see information on a Web site does not mean that it is accurate.

- **What person or organization established or maintains this Web site? What is the purpose of the site?** What makes this person or organization an expert?

- **What is the purpose of the site?** Whether a person or an organization maintains a site, there is the potential for bias. Does the person or organization want to inform, to sell something, or to present a certain point of view?

- **When was the site last updated?** Just as with print sources, the publication date may matter, depending on whether you need current information.

Write *yes* or *no* to indicate whether these sources would be reliable.

_____ You are writing about a recent natural disaster. You consult a report on the National Weather Service's Web site.

_____ You are writing about Egypt's pyramids and how they were built. You refer to an article in a history magazine that was published 18 years ago.

_____ You are writing an article about testing in schools. You go to your state's Department of Education Web site to collect data.

_____ You are writing an article on skateboard safety. You cite www.Kensboards.com, which is a site that sells custom-make skateboards.

Helping at Home

Do an Internet search about a topic of your child's choice. Examine two or three Web sites from the search results using the criteria given on this page. Which is the most reliable source?

Graphics and Visual Aids

What is a picture worth? If you're putting together a bike, a picture to go along with the instructions can make the difference between success and failure. Sometimes, words can only do so much. Then, you need a picture to help out. Pictures can be drawings, photographs, maps, graphs, or diagrams.

The visual aid below shows a great deal of information, which saves the writer a lot of work.

A recent news article criticized the amount of money that Jennings County Schools spends on fuel and transportation. It is a fact that we spend 15% more on fuel and transportation than neighboring school districts. The reason is because our school district covers a wider area than most other school districts.

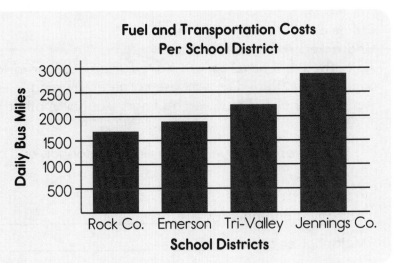

Graph the data below to help the Jennings County school superintendent prove that Jennings County has more students than nearby schools and, therefore, needs more money for school lunches. Use a bar graph similar to the one above.

School District	Enrollment
Jennings Co.	25,494 students
Emerson	17,239 students
Tri-Valley	16,117 students
Rock Co.	22,876 students

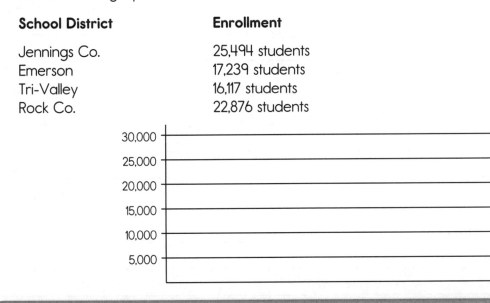

Suggest that your child use software and Internet tools to create graphics and visual aids that provide information about a meaningful topic. The graphics could show how many items are in a collection or where your child might like to live someday.

Describing Characters

When you write a story, your characters must seem like real people. You need to let your reader know not only how they look but how they act, what they look like, and how they feel. You could just tell the reader that a character is friendly, scared, or angry, but your story will be more interesting if you show these feelings by the characters' actions.

Example:
Character: A frightened child
Adjectives and adverbs: red-haired, freckled, scared, lost, worried
Simile: as frightened as a mouse cornered by a cat
Action: He peeked between his fingers, but his mother was nowhere in sight.

Write adjectives and adverbs, a simile or metaphor, and an action to describe each character.

1. an angry woman

   Adjectives and adverbs: _____

   Metaphor or simile: _____

   Action: _____

2. a disappointed man

   Adjectives and adverbs: _____

   Metaphor or simile: _____

   Action: _____

3. a tired boy

   Adjectives and adverbs: _____

   Metaphor or simile: _____

   Action: _____

4. a hungry child

   Adjectives and adverbs: _____

   Metaphor or simile: _____

   Action: _____

Helping at Home

Read what your child wrote about each character. Pick your favorite and ask your child to think more about that character. What kind of story might include the character? What might his or her name be? How might the character dress?

Describing Setting

Where and when a story takes place is called the **setting**. You can tell about a setting, or you can show what the setting is like. Compare these pairs of sentences.

The sun was shining.
The glaring sun made my eyes burn.

The bus was crowded.
Paige shouldered her way down the aisle, searching for an empty seat on the crowded bus.

If you give your readers a clear picture of your story's setting, they'll feel as if they're standing beside your characters. Include words that describe the sights, sounds, smells, feel, and even taste if appropriate.

Write two sentences for each setting, clearly describing it for readers.

1. an empty kitchen early in the morning _____

_____

_____

2. a locker room after a basketball game _____

_____

_____

3. a dark living room during a scary TV movie _____

_____

_____

4. a classroom on the first day of school _____

_____

_____

Helping at Home

Have your child give you clues that describe a place you both know. Can you guess the place? Take turns describing places and guessing. Pick your favorite place from the game and imagine a story that might take place there.

Transition Words

Transition words help readers know when things happen and in what order. Here are some common transition words.

after	as soon as	before	during	finally	first
later	meanwhile	next	soon	then	when

Here is a paragraph from a personal narrative. Circle the transition words when you find them.

A week later, the glasses were ready. I guess I had gotten used to the idea. I was kind of eager. As soon as they were on, I said, "Hey, wow!" I could read a sign all the way across the street! I had had no idea the glasses would make such a huge difference. Then, I grinned up at my parents. "This girl can see perfectly fine," I announced.

Think about your morning routine. What do you do from the time you wake up until you get to school? Write this sequence of events in a paragraph. Remember that it is important to use transition words, but don't start every sentence with one. Use different sentence styles to keep your writing interesting.

_____

_____

_____

_____

_____

_____

_____

_____

_____

Helping at Home

Ask your child to tell a story about something that happened to him or her today. Hold up a finger each time he or she uses a transition word. Tell your child a story and ask him or her to count your transition words.

© Carson-Dellosa • CD-704506

Writing Dialogue

Dialogue is the conversation among characters in a story. Good dialogue helps readers get to know the characters. It also keeps the action of the story moving. Here is what dialogue looks like.

> The Chairman looked thoughtfully out the window. "Morgan seemed a little distracted," he said. "I hope he's alright."
> Smiling, Kip replied, "Oh, I'm sure he is, sir."
> "How far did he say he was going?" asked the Chairman.
> Kip checked a chart. "To Monroe Flats, sir."
> "Monroe Flats!" burst the Chairman. "He's walking?"
> "Yes, sir," said Kip, a little surprised at the Chairman's outburst. "He likes to walk," Kip added, thinking it might calm his boss. It didn't.
> "Is he mad?" ranted the Chairman. "No one knows what's out there. Send a patrol in a transport module to get him. Right away."

What do you learn about the Chairman from this dialogue?

_____

What do you learn about Kip?

_____

Take a closer look at a line of dialogue and its punctuation.

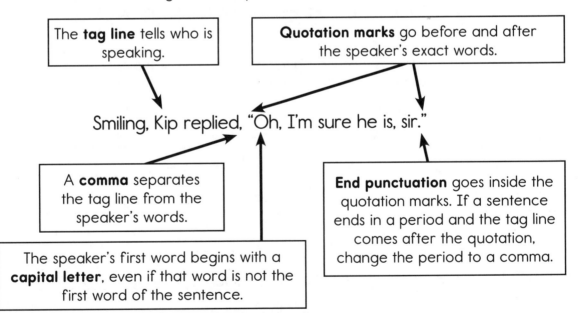

The **tag line** tells who is speaking.

Quotation marks go before and after the speaker's exact words.

Smiling, Kip replied, "Oh, I'm sure he is, sir."

A **comma** separates the tag line from the speaker's words.

End **punctuation** goes inside the quotation marks. If a sentence ends in a period and the tag line comes after the quotation, change the period to a comma.

The speaker's first word begins with a **capital letter**, even if that word is not the first word of the sentence.

Helping at Home

Ask your child to write several lines of dialogue from a favorite movie or TV show. Remind your child to punctuate the sentences correctly using the hints on this page as a guide. Can you guess the movie or TV show?

Pronouns

A **pronoun** is a word used in place of a noun.

A **subject pronoun** can be the subject of a sentence.
I, you, he, she, and *it* are subject pronouns.

I found the ball.   *You* found the ball.
He found the ball.   *She* found the ball.
It is my favorite sport.

An **object pronoun** can be the object of a sentence.
Me, you, him, her, and *it* are object pronouns.

Matt gave the ball to *me*.   Matt gave the ball to *you*.
Matt gave the ball to *him*.   Matt gave the ball to *her*.
Matt threw *it*.

Possessive pronouns show possession.
My, mine, your, yours, his, her, hers, and *its* are possessive pronouns.

Anna gave *my* ball to Matt.
Anna gave *mine* to Matt.

The plural forms of personal pronouns include:

Subject: *we, you, they*   *We/You/They* found the ball.
Object: *us, you, them*   Matt gave the ball to *us/you/them*.
Possessive: *our, ours, your, yours, their, theirs*
Matt gave *our ball/ours/your ball/yours/their ball/theirs* to Anna.

Complete the following sentences by choosing the best word in parentheses. Then, write what type of pronoun (subject, object, or possessive) it is on the line after the sentences.

1. _____ (I, Me) like movies. _____

2. Gloria handed the flowers to _____ (his, her) sister. _____

3. Stephanie wanted _____ (him, he) to ask her to the dance. _____

4. The teacher gave John _____ (his, her) paper back. _____

5. _____ (It, You) is the team's favorite food. _____

6. _____ (Him, You) are the quarterback on the football team. _____

7. The teacher wanted _____ (me, he) to try out for the play. _____

8. _____ (Her, She) likes volleyball better than softball. _____

Helping at Home

Many students mix up the possessive pronoun *its* (*The shirt lost its button*) and the contraction *it's* (*It's time to wake up*). Encourage your child to read a chapter of a favorite book and look for examples of these words. Are they used correctly?

Pronouns

The following skit contains subject, object, and possessive plural pronouns. Identify what each boldfaced plural pronoun is replacing on the line. Then, write whether the pronoun is a subject, object, or possessive on the line. The first one has been done for you.

Matt and Anna are on **their** _____Matt and Anna, possessive_____ way to the park to play.

On the way, **they** _____ meet Andrew and Stephanie.

"**We** _____ are on **our**

_____ way to the park," said Matt. "Can **you**

_____ join **us** _____?"

"Can **we** _____ play with **your**

_____ ball?" asked Stephanie. "**Ours**

_____ is missing."

"**Yours** _____ is missing? That's too bad," said

Anna. "Sure, **you** _____ can play with **our**

_____ ball."

Matt, Anna, Andrew, and Stephanie all walked to the park. They would all play together.

"I'll throw the ball to you," said Matt to Andrew. Then, you can throw the ball to **them**

_____," Matt said pointing to Anna and Stephanie.

"Hey," yelled Anna. "I see a ball ahead. Could it be Andrew and Stephanie's ball?"

"Yes, it could be **their**

_____

ball," answered Matt. Matt showed Andrew and

Stephanie the ball. Sure enough, it was **theirs**

_____.

© Carson-Dellosa • CD-704506

The pronoun *I* is used as part of the subject of a sentence (*I am going now*) and the pronoun *me* is used as part of the object of a sentence (*They invited me*). Think of more sentences with *I* and *me* to help your child practice this tricky skill.

Pronouns

Intensive pronouns add emphasis to the subject of a sentence. They are usually found right after the nouns or pronouns they modify. Here is a test to see if a pronoun is intensive. If it can be removed from a sentence and the sentence still makes sense, it is likely an intensive pronoun. Look at these examples:

I myself made the cake.

We went to hear the author herself read the book.

James himself bought the first ticket.

Complete each sentence below with one of these intensive pronouns: *myself, yourself, himself, herself, itself, ourselves, yourselves, themselves.*

1. Felicity _____ led the Fourth of July parade.

2. Do you _____ have any ideas for ways to recruit new players for our team?

3. After seeing the show in New York City, I had the chance to meet the actors _____.

4. The base is short, but the statue _____ is very tall.

5. I _____ decided weeks ago how I will vote in the election.

6. Though the artist's paintings are bold and passionate, the man _____ is said to be timid and shy.

7. They _____ will have to determine which parts of the building to repair.

8. As for we _____ , we all want to stay home on Saturday and go to the beach on Sunday.

After completing the page, ask your child to go back and circle the noun or pronoun in each sentence that provides the clue to the correct intensive pronoun. For example, in item #1, your child would circle *Felicity.*

Helping at Home

Pronouns

The noun that a pronoun refers to is called its **antecedent**. The word *antecedent* means "going before." If the noun is singular, the pronoun that takes its place must also be singular. If the noun is plural, the pronoun that takes its place must also be plural. This is called **agreement** between the pronoun and its antecedent.

Examples:
Mary (singular noun) said **she** (singular pronoun) would dance.
The **children** (plural noun) took **their** (plural pronoun) dishes outside.

When the noun is singular and the gender unknown, it is correct to use *his or her*.

After you!

Rewrite the sentences so the pronouns and nouns agree. The first one has been done for you.

1. Every student opened their book.

   Every student opened his or her book. _____

2. Has anyone lost their wallet lately?

   _____

3. Somebody found the wallet under their desk.

   _____

4. Someone will have to file their report.

   _____

5. Every dog has their day!

   _____

6. I felt Ted had mine best interests at heart.

   _____

Helping at Home

A common language error can be seen in the incorrect sentence *Each student picked their favorite.* Help your child understand that in formal writing, the sentence should be *Each student picked his or her favorite* or *Students picked their favorites.*

Pronouns

Write a pronoun that agrees with the antecedent.

1. Donald said _____ would go to the store.

2. My friend Leo discovered _____ wallet had been stolen.

3. The cat licked _____ paw.

4. Did any woman here lose _____ necklace?

5. Someone will have to give _____ report.

6. Jennifer wished _____ had not come.

7. All the children decided _____ would attend.

8. My grandmother hurt _____ back while gardening.

9. Jerry, Marco, and I hope _____ win the game.

10. Sandra looked for _____ missing homework.

11. The family had _____ celebration.

12. My dog jumps out of _____ pen.

13. Somebody needs to remove _____ clothes from this chair.

14. Everything has _____ place in Grandma's house.

15. The team will receive _____ uniforms on Monday.

16. Each artist wants _____ painting to win the prize.

When proofreading formal writing, it is important to make sure that nouns and pronouns agree. When your child proofreads writing for school, show how to find each pronoun used, then look back in the text to find the noun it should agree with.

© Carson-Dellosa • CD-704506

Avoiding Double Negatives

A **negative** sentence states the opposite. Negative words include *not*, *no*, *never*, *nobody*, *nowhere*, *nothing*, *barely*, *hardly*, and *scarcely*; and contractions containing the word *not*.

Double negatives happen when two negative words are used in the same sentence. Don't use double negatives; it will make your sentence positive again, and it is poor grammar.

Negative: We *won't* go anywhere without you.
Double Negative: We *won't* go *nowhere* without you.

Negative: I can *hardly* wait until baseball season.
Double Negative: I *can't hardly* wait until baseball season.

Rewrite the following sentences. Correct the sentence if it contains a double negative.

1. I love breakfast; I can't imagine not skipping it.

_____

2. I can't scarcely believe I made it all the way down the slope without falling.

_____

3. Samantha doesn't never like to wear her coat outside.

_____

4. The class hasn't received their report cards yet.

_____

5. I'm not going nowhere until it stops raining.

_____

6. Paul has barely nothing to contribute to the argument.

_____

7. Sarah never reveals her secrets.

_____

8. I don't think nobody can make it to the event early.

_____

Helping at Home

Begin a discussion with your child about the differences between informal speech and writing and formal speech and writing. When is it appropriate to use each type of communication? Why is it important to know the rules for formal language?

Appositives

An **appositive** is a noun or pronoun placed after another noun or pronoun to further identify or rename it. An appositive and the words that go with it are usually set off from the rest of the sentence with commas. Commas are not used if the appositive tells "which one."

Example: Angela's mother, Ms. Glover, will visit our school.

Commas are needed because *Ms. Glover* renames Angela's mother.

Example: Angela's neighbor Joan will visit our school.

Commas are not needed because *Joan* tells **which** neighbor.

Write the appositive in each sentence in the blank.
The first one has been done for you.

_____Tina_____   1. My friend Tina wants a horse.

_____   2. She subscribes to the magazine *Horses*.

_____   3. Her horse is the gelding "Brownie."

_____   4. We rode in her new car, a convertible.

_____   5. Her gift was jewelry, a bracelet.

_____   6. Have you met Ms. Abbott, the senator?

_____   7. My cousin Karl is very shy.

_____   8. Do you eat the cereal Oaties?

_____   9. Kiki's cat, Samantha, will eat only tuna.

_____   10. My last name, Jones, is very common.

Helping at Home

Encourage your child to write five sentences about himself or herself that include descriptive appositives. For example, if your daughter were Jordan, she might write: *Jordan, a sixth-grader at Watson School, is a member of the choir.*

Using Parentheses

Parentheses are used to show supplementary material, to set off phrases in a stronger way than commas, and to enclose numbers.

Supplementary material is a word or phrase that gives additional information.
    Theresa's mother *(the dentist)* will speak to our class next week.

Sometimes, words or phrases that might be set off with commas are set off with parentheses instead. It gives the information more emphasis for a stronger phrase.
    Leo's apartment building, *the one with the nice window boxes,* was voted prettiest in the neighborhood.
    Leo's apartment building *(the one with the nice window boxes)* was voted prettiest in the neighborhood.

Parentheses are also used to enclose numbers.
    Jacklyn wants to join the track team because *(1)* it is good exercise, *(2)* she can travel to other schools and cities, and *(3)* she can meet new friends.

Match the sentences in Column A with the reason why parentheses are used in Column B.

Column A	**Column B**
1. When cooking rice, don't forget to (1) rinse the rice, (2) steam the rice, and (3) eat the rice!	supplementary material
	set-off with emphasis
2. The preliminary findings (announced yesterday) are important to the study.	enclose numbers
3. The dinosaur bones (a huge discovery) can be seen in the museum.	
4. The orientation (for freshman) is this weekend.	supplementary material
5. Mac must (1) wash the dishes, (2) do his homework, and (3) get ready for bed.	set-off with emphasis
	enclose numbers
6. We're setting up our lemonade stand (the one that made $100 last summer) Memorial Day weekend.	

Helping at Home

When parentheses are used correctly, the parentheses and the words they contain can be removed and the sentence should still make sense. Encourage your child to try this test with the sentences on this page.

Using Dashes

Dashes (—) are used to indicate sudden changes of thought.

Examples:
I want milk—no, make that soda—with my lunch.
Wear your old clothes   new ones would get spoiled.

If the dash is used correctly in the sentence, write **C** in the blank. If the dash is missing or used incorrectly, draw an **X** in the blank. The first one has been done for you.

_____C_____ 1. No one—not even my dad—knows about the surprise.

_____ 2. Ask—him—no I will to come to the party.

_____ 3. I'll tell you the answer oh, the phone just rang!

_____ 4. Everyone thought—even her brother—that she looked pretty.

_____ 5. Can you please—oh, forget it!

_____ 6. Just stop it I really mean it!

_____ 7. Tell her that I'll—never mind—I'll tell her myself!

_____ 8. Everyone especially Anna is overwhelmed.

_____ 9. I wish everyone could—with a little help—follow their dreams.

_____ 10. The kids—all six of them—piled into the backseat.

Write two sentences of your own that include dashes.

11. _____

_____

12. _____

_____

Helping at Home
Encourage your child to experiment with a keyboard and word processing software to practice typing hyphens and dashes. Is a special keystroke needed to produce a long dash? Sometimes, two hyphens are used together to represent a dash.

Finding Spelling Errors

One word in each sentence below is misspelled. Write the word correctly on the line.

1. Jeff felt discoraged at the comparison between him and his older brother. _____

2. I got inpatient as my curiosity grew. _____

3. She confided that she had not finished the asignment. _____

4. They made the selection after a brief conferrence. _____

5. Obviusly, it's impolite to sneeze on someone. _____

6. This skin cream is practicaly invisible. _____

7. What would prevent you from taking on addtional work? _____

8. I can resite the words to that hymn. _____

9. In a previous columm, the newspaper explained the situation. _____

10. He decieved me so many times that now I distrust him. _____

11. Please have the curtesy to observe the "No Eating" signs. _____

12. The advertisement is so small that it's nearly invisble. _____

13. The best way to communicate is in a face-to-face conservation. _____

14. In a cost comparson, salmon is more expensive than tuna. _____

15. Poplarity among friends shouldn't depend on your accomplishments. _____

16. Her campaign was quite an acheivement. _____

17. He condemmed it as a poor imitation. _____

Helping at Home

Encourage your child to keep a list of words that he or she finds difficult to spell. This list might begin with these commonly misspelled words: *address, beautiful, especially, friend, receive, straight, tomorrow, weigh.*

Sentence Variety

Combining short, choppy sentences into longer more detailed sentences makes writing much more interesting and easier to read. Sentences can be combined in a variety of ways.

Compound Subjects and Compound Verbs:
The lightning is coming. The thunder is coming.
The *thunder and lightning* are coming.

Adjectives and Adverbs:
I went to a party. The party was a costume party.
I went to a *costume party.*

Making Complex Sentences (using subordinate conjunctions):
Donna wanted to go to the reunion. Diane did not want to go.
Donna wanted to go to the reunion, but Diane did not want to go.

Under Column A are five combined sentences. Under Column B are the parts of speech that were combined. Match the sentences in Column A with the parts of speech in Column B.

Column A

1. The salesman reluctantly attended the seminar.

2. Dan and Rose are taking swimming lessons.

3. Cam's parents lived in a beautiful neighborhood.

4. David climbed and descended the mountain.

5. The phone rang, but we were eating.

Column B

combined subjects

combined verbs

combined adjective and noun

combined adverb and verb

subordinate conjunction

Invite your child to read a page from a favorite book out loud to you. Then, notice together how the author uses sentences with different lengths and different patterns, making the text interesting to read. Compliment your child's reading!

Root Words

When you know what part of a word means, you may be able to figure out the meaning of the rest of the word. For example, *duct*, which means "to lead," is the root of *conduct* or *induct*. Look at the chart below. It has several root words and their meanings.

Root	Meaning	Example	Definition
act	to do	interact	to act with others
aqua	water	aquatint	dyed water
auto	self	automobile	to move oneself
centi	a hundred	centennial	one hundred years

Look at each word equation below. The meaning of one part is shown in parentheses. Consult the chart of root words to find the meaning of the other part. Write the meaning in the blank. Combine the two meanings. Write the dictionary definition in the space provided. The first one is done for you.

1. *react*   re (again) + act _____to do_____ = _____again to do_____

   Dictionary definition: __To act or do again_____

2. *automatic*   auto _____ + matic (having a mind) = _____

   Dictionary definition: _____

3. *transact*   trans (across) + act _____ = _____

   Dictionary definition: _____

4. *centimeter*   centi _____ + meter (meter) = _____

   Dictionary definition: _____

5. *aquanaut*   aqua _____ + naut (sailor) = _____

   Dictionary definition: _____

Choose one of the root words on this page. With your child, brainstorm a list of words that include it. For the root *aqua*, your list might include *aquifer*, *aquamarine*, *aquarium*, and *aquatic*. How does each relate to the meaning of the root, "water"?

Root Words

Root	Meaning	Example	Definition
cede	to go	supercede	to go beyond
cept	seize	intercept	to seize during
duce	lead	deduce	to find the lead
fer	carry	interfere	to carry into
port	carry	transport	to carry across
spect	to look	inspect	to look in
tain	to hold	obtain	to gain by action
vene	to come	convene	to come to start

Complete the exercises below. The first one is done for you.

1. *precede*   pre (before) + cede _____to go_____ = _____before to go_____

   Dictionary definition:__To be, go, or come before_____

2. *report*   re (again) + port _____ = _____

   Dictionary definition:_____

3. *intervene*   inter (between) + vene _____ = _____

   Dictionary definition:_____

4. *induce*   in (in) + duce _____ = _____

   Dictionary definition:_____

5. *retrospect*   retro (backward) + spect _____ = _____

   Dictionary definition:_____

6. *refer*   re (again) + fer _____ = _____

   Dictionary definition:_____

7. *retain*   re (again) + tain _____ = _____

   Dictionary definition:_____

Encourage your child to draw a plant with a long root and several leaves. On the root, write a root word such as *port*. On the leaves, write related words such as *transport, airport, export, portable,* and *support.*

Greek Roots

Many words in the English language have **Greek roots**. Learning the meanings of these roots can help you determine the meanings of some unfamiliar words.

chron = time	(**chron**ic)	**man** = hand	(**man**uscript)
bio = life	(**bio**logy)	**cycl** = circle, ring	(**cycl**one)
phon = sound	(tele**phon**e)	**therm** = heat	(**therm**al)

Read the clues below. Choose the word from the box that matches each clue and write it on the line.

biography   thermos   homophones   manual   tricycle   chronological   Cyclops

1. arranged by order of time _____

2. words that sound the same but are spelled differently _____

3. the story of a person's life _____

4. a vehicle that has three circular wheels _____

5. to do something by hand _____

6. a bottle that keeps liquids hot _____

7. a creature from Greek mythology that has one round eye _____

Read the sentences below. Underline the word from the pair in parentheses that correctly completes each sentence.

1. Beachwood Middle School won an award for (cycling, recycling) more materials than any other school in the county.

2. Maddy treasures her grandfather's diary because it (chronicles, chronic) his journey to America and his first years in this country.

3. My parents always turn down the (thermostat, thermometer) at night.

Encourage your child to read Greek myths and learn about ancient Greek gods such as Atlas, Fortuna, Vulcan, and Mars. How do their stories relate to English words such as *atlas, fortune, volcano,* and *martial?*

Latin Roots

Like Greek roots, **Latin roots** can help you determine the meanings of unfamiliar words.

aud = hear	(**aud**ible)	**ann, enn** = year	(**ann**iversary)
vid, vis = see	(**vid**eo)	**liber** = free	(**liber**ate)
mar = sea	(sub**mar**ine)	**aqua** = water	(**aqua**tic)
ped = foot	(**ped**estal)		

Circle the word that matches each definition below.

1. occurring once a year

    biennial   annual   aquatic

2. a large room where people go to hear or see a performance

    auditorium   audience   revision

3. freedom

    liberal   liberty   impede

4. an insect that has many pairs of legs

    pedestrian   aqueduct   millipede

5. a color of bluish-green that looks like water

    aquamarine   marine   mariner

6. nautical; of or relating to the sea

    submarine   liberate   maritime

7. the part of a bicycle that is operated by the foot

    pedestal   pedal   peddler

Helping at Home

Encourage your child to learn about Latin, the language of ancient Rome. It is the origin of many languages. These words mean "good": *bonus* (Latin), *bonne* (French), *buono* (Italian), *bueno* (Spanish). Can your child find more examples of words from Latin?

Using a Dictionary

When you look up a word in a dictionary, you are looking up an **entry word**. Entry words, which are usually printed in bold, are often base words. For example, you would look for *pretty*, not *prettier*, and *silly*, not *silliness*.

entry word	pronunciation & syllables	part of speech	meaning

laboratory (lab′ rə tȯr′ē) *noun* a room in which scientific research and experiments are done

Write the entry word beside each bold word below.

1. **crickets** _____

2. **contains** _____

3. **rubbing** _____

4. **dragonflies** _____

5. **divided** _____

6. **mosquitoes** _____

7. **found** _____

8. **soaring** _____

Use the dictionary entries below to answer the questions that follow.

sincere (sin sêr′) *adj.* honest; genuine, *noun* sincerity
squash (skwosh) **1.** *noun* a fruit that is related to pumpkins and gourds
　　　　　　 2. *verb* to crush or press flat
refrigerator (ri frij′ ə rā tər) *noun* a machine or appliance that keeps food cold

1. On the line below, write a sentence using the word *squash* as a verb.

_____

2. Which is an entry word—*sincere* or *sincerity*? _____

3. Which guide words would you find on the same page as *refrigerator*?

reef • refresh　　　reflection • regal　　　refugee • rehearse　_____

4. How many syllables are there in *refrigerator*? _____

Make sure your child has access to a dictionary, either a print version on an online version. Practice and model dictionary skills by keeping a dictionary handy when you read, watch news or documentary programs on TV, or play word games.

Helping at Home

Figurative Language: Metaphors

A **metaphor** is a comparison of two unlike things without using *like* or *as*.

Example: The *buttercups were a colorful blanket* spread across the yard.

On the lines, tell which two things in each metaphor are being compared.

1. The leaves of the seedlings were tiny hands reaching toward the sun.

   _____   _____

2. The three golf balls Preston found were perfectly round eggs nestled in the high grasses beside the pond.

   _____   _____

3. Once the Nelsons lost power, their house quickly became an icebox.

   _____   _____

4. The little white dog's tail was a flag waving proudly in spite of the rain.

   _____   _____

5. For the kids, the seashells were tiny treasures strewn along the beach.

   _____   _____

6. When Davis put on his hockey uniform, he became a warrior heading into battle.

   _____   _____

7. The lights of the city were a constellation speckling the night sky.

   _____   _____

Helping
at Home

Ask your child to think of an everyday activity such as loading the dishwasher or putting on socks. Have fun together thinking of dramatic and silly metaphors to describe the activity.

Figurative Language: Personification

When an author gives an object or animal human characteristics, it is called **personification**.

Example: The dragon quickly *thought* out its next move in the attack on the village.

Thought is a human process and not associated with mythical creatures; therefore, the dragon is personified in that sentence.

In the following sentences, underline the personification.

1. The cave's gaping mouth led to internal passageways.

2. The tractor sprang to life with a turn of the key.

3. The lights blinked twice and then died.

4. Crops struggled to survive in the blistering heat, hoping for rainfall.

5. The engine of the car coughed and sputtered as if it wanted to breathe but couldn't.

6. The arrow flew through the air, eyeing its target.

7. Snowmen smile from the safety of their yards.

8. Four-year-old Stephanie's doll sipped tea delicately.

Write a sentence that personifies the following objects.

1. flower_____

2. stuffed animal_____

3. car_____

Helping at Home

Ask your child to search for and read a copy of the poem "the sky is low" by Emily Dickinson. How does it use personification?

Analogies

An **analogy** shows a relationship between two pairs of words. To understand an analogy, it is important to figure out how the words relate to one another.

Examples:
- *Bored* Is to *excited* as *wide* is to *narrow*.
    Bored is an antonym for *excited* as *wide* is an antonym for *narrow*.
- *Wheel* is to *car* as *page* is to *book*.
    A wheel is part of a car, just as a page is part of a book.
- *Bird* is to *nest* as *horse* is to *stable*.
    A nest is the home of a bird, just as a stable is the home of a horse.

To read an analogy written in the following format—puppy : dog :: lamb : sheep—you would say, "*Puppy* is to *dog* as *lamb* is to *sheep*."

The analogies below are incomplete. Underline the word from the pair in parentheses that best completes each analogy.

1. (Increase, Reduce) is to *decrease* as *question* is to *answer*.

2. *Sprinkle* is to *sprinkling* as (copied, copy) is to *copying*.

3. *Mitten* is to *hand* as *sock* is to (finger, foot).

4. *Nickel* is to *dollar* as (second, hour) is to *minute*.

5. (Never, Often) is to *frequently* as *vanish* is to *disappear*.

6. (September, March) is to *April* as *breakfast* is to *lunch*.

7. *Athlete* is to *team* as (student, principal) is to *class*.

8. *Eight* is to *ate* as *carats* is to (carrots, vegetables).

9. *Refrigerator* is to (food, stove) as *closet* is to *clothing*.

10. *Vacuum* is to (sponge, cleaning) as *trowel* is to *gardening*.

11. *Forty-two* is to (twenty-four, twenty-two) as *sixty-one* is to *sixteen*.

12. *Ballet* is to *dance* as *piano* is to (trombone, instrument).

13. *Lemon* is to *sour* as *chocolate* is to (sweet, cake).

Helping at Home

To solve an analogy, figure out the relationship between the two given words. Then, choose a word that establishes the same relationship between the second pair of words. Write a challenging analogy for your child to solve. Try to stump each other.

Analogies

Complete each analogy below with a word from the box. Remember to figure out how the words are related before you look for the missing word.

web   seedling   sport   princess   lead   patients   Detroit   bracelet

1. New Mexico : state :: _____ : city

2. cards : game :: basketball : _____

3. _____ : mislead :: zero : subzero .

4. king : queen :: prince : _____

5. spider : _____ :: architect : house

6. _____ : plant :: fall : winter

7. earring : ear :: _____ : wrist

8. _____ : patience :: sundae : Sunday

Read each analogy below. Decide which category in the box it matches and write the letter of the category on the line.

a. Part–Whole Relationship
b. Object–Use Relationship
c. Numerical Relationship
d. Grammatical Relationship
e. Object–Place Relationship
f. Synonym or Antonym Relationship

1. _____ *Cactus* is to *desert* as *skier* is to *mountain.*

2. _____ *Slice* is to *pizza* as *button* is to *shirt.*

3. _____ *Attract* is to *repel* as *generous* is to *stingy.*

4. _____ *Book* is to *library* as *judge* is to *courthouse.*

5. _____ *Geese* is to *goose* as *marshmallows* is to *marshmallow.*

6. _____ *Seventy-three* is to *seventy-five* as *seventy-nine* is to *eighty-one.*

7. _____ *Scissors* is to *cut* as *mirror* is to *reflect.*

Helping at Home

Challenge your child to write a new analogy to illustrate each category in the box on the lower part of this page. Ask him or her to erase one word from each of the new analogies and see if you or another family member can complete them.

Denotations and Connotations

Sometimes, two words can be similar, yet you would not substitute one for the other because they each suggest different feelings.

Denotation means the literal or dictionary definition of a word. **Connotation** is the meaning of a word including all the emotions associated with it. For example, *job* and *chore* are synonyms, but because of their connotations, anyone would choose to do a job instead of a chore.

Circle the word in each group with the most positive connotation.

task	old	retort
job	mature	respond
chore	antiquated	react

remainder	haughty	conversational
remnants	cheeky	wordy
residue	proud	talkative

excessively	relaxed	shack
grossly	lazy	hovel
abundantly	inactive	hut

curious	swift	scamp
prying	hasty	rascal
nosy	speedy	hoodlum

Helping at Home

Ask your child to write an ad for selling something old and unwanted. It should be full of words with positive connotations. Next, write an ad for something treasured that your child does not really want to sell. It should be full of words with negative connotations.

Denotations and Connotations

Replace the bold word in each sentence with a word that has a more positive connotation.

Example:

~~shut~~
He **slammed** the door when he left.

The dog's energy was **uncontrollable**.

We hoped to settle our **fight** peacefully.

The mother **reprimanded** the children when people began to look at them.

The children **gossiped** at lunchtime.

The girl **scribbled** a hasty note to leave behind.

Our conversation ended **abruptly** when the phone rang.

The principal was a **severe** man.

The boy **snatched** the toy from his baby brother.

The couple **rejected** their offer of help.

Dad reminded me to clean my **disastrous** room.

Helping at Home

Watch a TV commercial with your child, looking for examples of connotative language. Urge your child to think critically about the ad's word choices and messages. What neutral words could take the place of connotative words?

Common Core State Standards for Math*

The following parent-friendly explanations of sixth grade Common Core math standards are provided to help you understand what your child will learn in school this year. Practice pages listed will help your child master each skill.

Complete Common Core State Standards may be found here: www.corestandards.org.

6.RP Ratios and Proportional Relationships

Understand ratio concepts and use ratio reasoning to solve problems.
(Standards: 6.RP.A.1, 6.RP.A.2, 6.RP.A.3a, 6.RP.A.3b, 6.RP.A.3c, 6.RP.A.3d)

Your child will write ratios to describe relationships between quantities. For example, he or she will write 2:1 to show that there are two cups of flour for every one cup of sugar.
• **Practice page: 68**

Your child will find unit rates. For example, given the fact that a runner travels six miles in two hours, your child will find the runner's rate of speed per hour. • **Practice pages: 69, 70**

Your child will understand ratios as sets of numbers that can be graphed or plotted on a coordinate plane. For example, when working with ratios about dollars saved each week, your child will create a graph showing weeks versus dollars saved and plot each amount.
• **Practice pages: 68, 71, 72**

Your child will understand percentage as a rate per 100. He or she will solve problems involving percentages. For example, given that 15 is 25% of a number, your child will find the whole number 60. • **Practice pages: 73–76**

Your child will apply an understanding of ratios to units of measurement. For example, he or she will use the ratio three feet per yard to convert eight yards into 24 feet.
• **Practice pages: 77, 78**

6.NS The Number System

Apply and extend previous understandings of multiplication and division to divide fractions by fractions.
(Standard: 6.NS.A.1)

Your child will solve problems that involve dividing fractions by fractions. He or she will be asked to solve word problems like this: How many $\frac{1}{2}$ cup servings are in $2\frac{2}{3}$ cups of yogurt?
• **Practice pages: 79–81**

Compute fluently with multi-digit numbers and find common factors and multiples.
(Standards: 6.NS.B.2, 6.NS.B.3, 6.NS.B.4)

Your child will build on his or her knowledge of division to divide multi-digit numbers by multi-digit numbers. For example, he or she might be asked to divide 11,610 by 132 without using a calculator. • **Practice pages: 82, 83**

Your child will expand on his or her understanding of place value to add, subtract, multiply, and divide numbers that include decimal points. He or she will learn how to make sure the decimal point is in the right place in a problem's solution. • **Practice pages: 84–87**

Your child will list factors of two numbers and identify the greatest common factor. For example, factors of 9 include 1, 3, and 9. Factors of 18 include 1, 2, 3, 6, 9, and 18. The greatest common factor of 9 and 18 is 9. Likewise, your child will find the least common multiple, or the smallest multiple shared by two numbers. The least common multiple of 9 and 18 is 18. • **Practice pages: 88, 89**

Apply and extend previous understandings of numbers to the system of rational numbers.
(Standards: 6.NS.C.5, 6.NS.C.6a, 6.NS.C.6b, 6.NS.C.6c, 6.NS.C.7a, 6.NS.C.7b, 6.NS.C.7c, 6.NS.C.7d)

Your child will understand that negative numbers such as –2 represent values below 0. Real-world examples include miles below sea level or negative bank account balances.
• **Practice pages: 90, 91**

Your child will find negative numbers on a number line and on the coordinate plane, compare positive and negative numbers, and recognize that positive and negative numbers like 3 and –3 are opposites. • **Practice pages: 90, 92**

Your child will learn that a number with vertical lines on either side is an absolute value. Absolute value is a number's distance away from 0 expressed as a positive number. So, |12| = 12 and |–12| = 12. • **Practice page: 93**

Common Core State Standards for Math*

6.EE Expressions and Equations

**Apply and extend previous understandings of arithmetic to algebraic expressions.
(Standards: 6.EE.A.1, 6.EE.A.2a, 6.EE.A.2b, 6.EE.A.2c, 6.EE.A.3, 6.EE.A.4)**

Your child will look at numbers that have exponents, such as 8^2, and understand that the exponent tells how many times to multiply a number by itself. So, $8^2 = 8 \times 8 = 64$.
• **Practice page: 95**

Your child will write simple algebraic expressions in which letters stand for numbers. For "add 8 to an unknown number," your child will write $8 + x$. In addition, your child will learn words such as variable, term, and coefficient to describe parts of an algebraic expression.
• **Practice pages: 96, 97**

Your child will evaluate expressions by plugging in specific values for variables. For example, what is $x + 8$ if $x = 2.5$? • **Practice page: 98**

Your child will practice using the order of operations, or the standard order for solving an equation like $5(13 - 3) = x$. First, solve all parts of the equation that are in brackets or parentheses. Second, do multiplications and divisions in the equation. Finally, do additions and subtractions. • **Practice page: 94**

Your child will understand that the distributive property combines addition and multiplication. It means that $3 \times (2 + 5)$ is the same as $(3 \times 2) + (3 \times 5)$. These expressions are equivalent.
• **Practice pages: 99, 100**

**Reason about and solve one-variable equations and inequalities.
(Standards: 6.EE.B.7, 6.EE.B.8)**

Your child will solve simple algebraic equations using addition, subtraction, multiplication, and division. • **Practice pages: 101, 102**

Your child will apply his or her knowledge of simple inequalities such as $6 + 5 > 10 - 2$ to solve algebraic inequalities that include variables. • **Practice pages: 103–105**

6.G Geometry

Solve real-world and mathematical problems involving area, surface area, and volume.
(Standards: 6.G.A.1, 6.G.A.2, 6.G.A.4)

Your child will find the area of triangles, quadrilaterals (four-sided shapes), and polygons using standard formulas. If necessary, your child will break down larger shapes into rectangles and triangles in order to calculate their area. • **Practice pages: 106–109**

Your child will find the volume of rectangular prisms, or box-like shapes. • **Practice page: 110**

Your child will use patterns of equal-sized squares, or "nets," to mentally construct three-dimensional shapes, think about the surfaces that make them up, and calculate their surface areas. • **Practice page: 111**

6.SP Statistics and Probability

Develop understanding of statistical variability.
(Standards: 6.SP.A.1, 6.SP.A.2, 6.SP.A.3)

Your child will ask statistical questions such as "How tall are the students in my class at school?" He or she will recognize that data gathered to answer these questions have a range of values that can be analyzed and shown in different ways. • **Practice pages: 112, 113**

Your child will understand that when statistical data is arranged in a distribution, it can be described by its middle value, range of values, and overall shape. For example, some data distributions form a bell-shaped curve. • **Practice pages: 114–116**

Summarize and describe distributions.
(Standards: 6.SP.B.4, 6.SP.B.5a, 6.SP.B.5b, 6.SP.B.5c, 6.SP.B.5d)

Your child will use data sets to create different types of graphs including dot plots, histograms, and box plots. He or she will use completed graphs to analyze the data and answer questions. • **Practice pages: 117–121**

Your child will work with data sets, looking at the overall shape of the data and finding the median (the middle value in a sorted list of data), the mean (the average, or center), the mode (the number or value that appears most often in a data set), and the range (the total spread of the data). • **Practice pages: 112–116**

Ratios and Proportions

A **ratio** is a comparison of two numbers. A ratio can be expressed as 1 to 2, 1:2, or $\frac{1}{2}$, and it means that for every 1 of the first item, there are 2 of the other item. For example, 2 dollars per gallon is a ratio. For every 1 gallon you buy, you pay 2 dollars.

A **proportion** expresses the equality of two ratios. To check if a proportion is true, cross-multiply to determine if the two ratios are equal.

$\frac{4}{2} \bowtie \frac{2}{1}$ $\frac{4}{2} = \frac{2}{1}$ $4 \times 1 = 2 \times 2$, so it is true. $\frac{3}{4} = \frac{2}{3}$ $3 \times 3 \neq 4 \times 2$, so it is **not** true.

Circle the proportions that are true. Show your work.

1. $\frac{1}{4} = \frac{2}{8}$ $\frac{1}{3} = \frac{4}{9}$ $\frac{2}{7} = \frac{6}{21}$

2. $\frac{9}{4} = \frac{27}{16}$ $\frac{3}{25} = \frac{12}{100}$ $\frac{4}{5} = \frac{12}{20}$

3. $\frac{1}{11} = \frac{3}{30}$ $\frac{8}{3} = \frac{24}{9}$ $\frac{15}{25} = \frac{3}{5}$

4. $\frac{8}{9} = \frac{72}{81}$ $\frac{7}{8} = \frac{49}{64}$ $\frac{11}{12} = \frac{20}{24}$

The picture, table, and graph below all illustrate the same ratio.

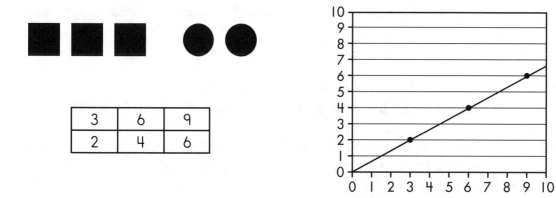

3	6	9
2	4	6

5. Which fraction expresses this ratio in simplest form? Circle the correct answer.

A. $\frac{3}{6}$ B. $\frac{3}{4}$ C. $\frac{3}{2}$

Helping at Home
During a car trip, assign passengers to count items seen in one mile. You might count red cars, semitrucks, billboards, or street signs. Then, express the counts as ratios. For example, how many red cars were counted for each blue car?

Unit Rate Problems

A **rate** is a ratio of two measurements that have different kinds of units. For example, if you drive 150 miles in 3 hours, miles and hours are different kinds of units. When a rate is simplified so that it has a denominator of 1, it is called a **unit rate**. For example, 50 miles per hour is a unit rate; it means 50 miles per 1 hour. The word *per* indicates a rate.

A package of 5 pads of paper costs $4.95. What is the unit rate?

$$\frac{4.95 \text{ dollars}}{5 \text{ pads of paper}} = \frac{0.99 \text{ dollars}}{1 \text{ pad}}$$ For the 5-pack of paper, the unit rate is $0.99 per pad.

Solve each problem.

1. A magazine subscription costs $47.40 for 12 issues. What is the price per issue?

   The price per issue is _____.

2. A 6-pack of sports drinks costs $7.50. What is the price per bottle?

   The price per bottle is _____.

3. The 30 members of a class are going on a field trip. The total cost of the trip is $457.50. What is the cost per student?

   The cost per student is _____.

4. Brian is visiting Britain and wants to exchange U.S. dollars for British pounds. The rate of exchange is 1 U.S. dollar = 0.65 British pound. How many British pounds will Brian get for 200 U.S. dollars?

   Brian will get _____ British pounds for 200 U.S. dollars.

Helping at Home

At the grocery store, ask your child to help you shop for laundry detergent, pet food, or other items based on the unit cost. Encourage your child to look for unit costs on store labels and verify them with his or her own calculations.

Unit Rate Problems

Solve each problem. Show your work.

1. Four boxes of grapefruit weigh 160 pounds. How many pounds are in 5 boxes?

2. A survey found that 2 out of 4 students take physical education. If 32 students take physical education, how many students were surveyed?

3. A supply store sells 5 pens for every 4 pencils. The store sold 25 pens yesterday. How many pencils did it sell?

4. On a map, each inch represents 20 miles. What is the actual length of an interstate highway if it is 4 inches long on the map?

5. There are 32 calculators in 4 boxes of calculators. How many calculators are there in 9 boxes?

6. If $1 U.S. equals 1.35 euros, how many euros does $20 U.S. equal?

7. A drawing of a fish has a scale of 12 centimeters to 3 centimeters. If the actual fish is 16 centimeters long, how long is the drawing?

Helping at Home

Encourage your child to research the dimensions of the Golden Gate Bridge, Mt. Everest, or another landmark. Can your child use what he or she knows about ratios to draw a scale model of the landmark?

Graphing Ratios

Any set of ordered pairs is a **relation**, because each pair relates two values. Think of the graph at right as Quadrant I of a coordinate plane. Tom deposits $10 into his savings account each week. The graph relates Tom's savings to the week.

The **domain** of a relation is all the x-values in the set. In this example, the domain is the set of values {1, 2, 3, 4, 5}. The **range** of a relation is all the y-values in the set. The range of this relation is {$10, $20, $30, $40, $50}.

Tom's Savings

(graph: Dollars on y-axis from 0 to 60, Week on x-axis from 0 to 6, points plotted at (1,10), (2,20), (3,30), (4,40), (5,50))

Week (x-values)	Dollars (y-values)
1	10
2	20
3	30
4	40
5	50

What is the ratio of dollars to weeks in Week 5? **5 weeks to $50**, or **1:10**. Is the ratio for Week 3 the same? **Yes. 3:30 = 1:10.** Draw a line connecting the points on the graph.

Solve this problem.

1. For her business, Carey's Roses, Carey buys a box of two dozen roses wholesale for $20. Make a table and graph of her costs for 2, 4, 6, and 8 boxes of roses. Be sure to label the x-axis and y-axis in your graph.

   What would Carey's cost be for 20 dozen roses? _____

Boxes (x values)	Dollars (y values)

**Carey's Roses
Wholesale Cost per Box**

(blank graph)

How old will your child be in the year 2025? 2036? Have your child make a list of dates and corresponding ages and plot the points on a graph.

Graphing Ratios

1. Bob and Jack went on a trip together driving separate cars. The table gives data from the 5 legs of their trip. They followed the same route at the same speed. Graph the 5 legs of their trip on the grid below. For each leg in the trip, mark a dot on the graph for Bob's gas use and an *x* on the graph for Jack's gas use.

Based on the graph, how did Jack's use of gas compare to Bob's?

_____

Leg	Distance Traveled (miles)	Bob's Gas Use (gallons)	Jack's Gas Use (gallons)
1	190	7	6.5
2	228	7.5	7
3	260	9	8.5
4	282	11.5	9.5
5	325	12.5	11.5

Bob and Jack's Gas Use

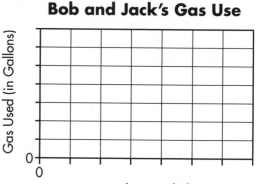

2. Ms. Rivera recorded her students' average study hours per week and course grade, as shown in the table. Make a graph of the data. Label the *x*- and *y*-axes.

Based on your graph, how are number of study hours related to grade?

_____

Student	Study Hours per Week	Course Grade
Sheree	5	98
Paul	1.5	60
Tom	4	90
Marcus	4.5	93
Linda	2	70
Alicia	3	84
Pat	2	65

Study Hours and Course Grade

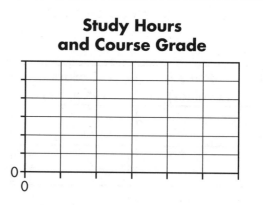

Help your child think of everyday situations that involve ratios. For example, the number of students who wear a jacket to school might be compared to the temperature outside. Encourage your child to collect and graph the ratios.

Finding Percentages

Percent (%) means "out of 100."

Examples: 1 percent (1%) = 0.01 = $\frac{1}{100}$. 125% = 1.25 = $1\frac{25}{100}$ = $1\frac{1}{4}$

Use this method to change a percent into a fraction:

$$12\% = \frac{12}{100} \div \frac{4}{4} = \frac{3}{25}$$

Use this method to change a fraction into a percent:

$$\frac{5}{8} = \frac{n}{100} \qquad 500 = 8n \qquad 62\frac{1}{2}\% = n$$

Use this method to change a decimal to a percent:

$$0.165 = \frac{16.5}{100} = 16.5\%$$

Use this method to change a percent to a decimal:

$$49.5\% = \frac{49.5}{100} = 0.495$$

For each fraction or mixed numeral, write the equivalent percent. For each percent, write the equivalent fraction or mixed numeral.

1. 20% = _____   _____% = $\frac{3}{8}$ 120% = _____

2. _____% = $2\frac{5}{8}$ 82% = _____ $14\frac{1}{4}$% = _____

3. 164% = _____   _____% = $\frac{7}{20}$ _____% = $\frac{4}{25}$

4. _____% = $\frac{19}{20}$ 248% = _____   _____% = $3\frac{3}{10}$

For each decimal, write the equivalent percent. For each percent, write the equivalent decimal.

5. 5.75% = _____   _____% = 0.125   58% = _____

6. _____% = 1.15   9% = _____   _____% = 0.035

7. 225% = _____   _____% = 0.005   99% = _____

8. _____% = 0.8   _____% = 3.82   52.25% = _____

Have your child read an interesting news or information article that includes percentages. Help him or her convert the percentages to fractions and decimals. How does manipulating the numbers help your child understand the article?

Finding Percentages

Examples:

35% of $60 = 35\% \times 60$
$$= \frac{35}{100} \times 60$$
$$= \frac{7}{20} \times \frac{60}{1} = \frac{420}{20} = \frac{42}{2}$$
$$= 21$$

40% of $32 = 40\% \times 32$
$$= \frac{40}{100} \times \frac{32}{1}$$
$$= \frac{2}{5} \times \frac{32}{1} = \frac{64}{5}$$
$$= 12\frac{4}{5}$$

Write each answer in simplest form.

1. 8% of $65 = $ _____ 95% of $80 = $ _____

2. 30% of $32 = $ _____ 25% of $28 = $ _____

3. 150% of $12 = $ _____ 25% of $30 = $ _____

4. 28% of $7 = $ _____ 10% of $38 = $ _____

5. 40% of $20 = $ _____ 15% of $45 = $ _____

6. 80% of $80 = $ _____ 20% of $75 = $ _____

7. 45% of $70 = $ _____ 18% of $45 = $ _____

8. 4% of $92 = $ _____ 16% of $90 = $ _____

9. 90% of $60 = $ _____ 25% of $86 = $ _____

10. 12% of $40 = $ _____ 9% of $60 = $ _____

11. 60% of $60 = $ _____ 95% of $20 = $ _____

12. 21% of $50 = $ _____ 3% of $25 = $ _____

Helping at Home

Encourage your child to shop online for three items he or she wants. How much does each cost? How much would each cost if it were 15% off? 20% off?

Finding Percentages

Example: 26% of 73.2   26% = 26 × 0.01 = 0.26

$$\begin{array}{r} 7\ 3.2 \\ \times\ \ 0.2\ 6 \\ \hline 4\ 3\ 9\ 2 \\ +\ 1\ 4\ 6\ 4\ \ \ \\ \hline 1\ 9.0\ 3\ 2 \end{array}$$

26% of 73.2 = 19.032

Complete the following.

1. 32% of 64 = _____   26% of 40 = _____

2. 2.5% of 89 = _____   1.2% of 385 = _____

3. 58% of 12 = _____   250% of 8 = _____

4. 73% of 8.4 = _____   49% of 86 = _____

5. 0.8% of 256 = _____   11% of 29 = _____

6. 120% of 35 = _____   7.5% of 60 = _____

7. 84% of 7 = _____   40% of 95 = _____

8. 20% of 45 = _____   22% of 142 = _____

9. 9.2% of 63 = _____   80% of 80 = _____

10. 7% of 112 = _____   62% of 45 = _____

Helping at Home

Help your child list the number of hours he or she spent doing various activities yesterday such as sleeping, eating, and attending school. What percentage of the 24-hour day did your child spend doing each activity?

Finding Percentages

Solve each problem.

1. The sales tax on the purchase of a refrigerator that costs $695 is 7 percent. What is the amount of sales tax?

   The sales tax is _____.

2. A stove that costs $695 will be on sale next week for 28 percent off its regular price. What is the amount of savings?

   The savings will be _____.

3. In math class, 60 percent of the students are males. There are 30 students in the class. How many students are males?

   There are _____ males.

4. East Side Middle School has 1,500 students. Thirty-two percent of them are in sixth grade. How many sixth-grade students are there?

   There are _____ sixth-grade students.

5. Lauren is saving for gymnastics camp. Camp costs $225 to attend. She has 40 percent of the money saved. How much money has she saved?

   Lauren has saved _____.

6. Of the 1,500 students attending East Side Middle School, twenty-five percent are running for student council. How many students are running for student council?

   _____ students are running for student council.

Helping at Home

Ask your child to think about how to spend an imaginary $1,000. What items would he or she buy? About what percentage of the money would be spent on each item?

Converting Measurements

1 foot (ft.) = 12 inches (in.)   1 in. = $\frac{1}{12}$ ft.
1 yard (yd.) = 3 ft.   1 ft. = $\frac{1}{3}$ yd.
1 yd. = 36 in.   1 in. = $\frac{1}{36}$ yd.
1 mile (mi.) = 5,280 ft.   1 mi. = 1,760 yd.

24 in. = _____ ft.   5 ft. 8 in. = _____ in.
1 in. = $\frac{1}{12}$ ft.   1 ft. = 12 in.
24 in. = (24 × $\frac{1}{12}$) ft.   5 ft. = (5 × 12) or 60 in.
24 in. = ___2___ ft.   5 ft. 8 in. = (60 + 8) in.
                                       5 ft. 8 in. = ___68___ in.

Complete the following.

1.   7 ft. = _____ in.   72 in. = _____ ft.   15 yd. = _____ ft.

2.   108 in. = _____ yd.   4 mi. = _____ ft.   4 mi. = _____ yd.

3.   3 yd. = _____ ft.   120 in. = _____ ft.   42 ft. = _____ yd.

4.   4 ft. 7 in. = _____ in. 2 yd 9 in. = _____ in.   30 in. = _____ ft.

5.   15,840 ft. = _____ mi.   6 yd. = _____ ft.   6 yd. = _____ in.

6.   7 yd. 2 ft. = _____ ft. 7 yd. 2 ft. = _____ in. 24 ft. = _____ yd.

7.   11 ft. 9 in. = _____ in. 2 mi. 500 ft. = _____ ft. 52,800 ft. = _____ mi.

8.   25 ft. = _____ in.   144 in. = _____ ft.   144 in. = _____ yd.

9.   5 mi. = _____ yd.   18 in. = _____ ft.   12 yd. = _____ ft.

10. 12 yd. = _____ in.   2,640 ft. = _____ mi.   5 yd. 8 in. = _____ in.

Ask your child to find the distance in miles from your home to a nearby place such as school or a friend's house. Have your child convert that distance to yards, feet, and inches. Do the same exercise with a faraway place.

Converting Measurements

Metric units of weight are **milligrams** (mg), **grams** (g), and **kilograms** (kg).

Examples:

63 kg = _____ g
1 kg = 1000 g
63 kg = (63 × 1000) g
63 k = 63000 g

32 mg = _____ g
1 mg = 0.001 g
32 mg = (32 × 0.001) g
32 mg = 0.032 g

> 1 g = 1000 mg
> 1 kg = 1000 g
> 1 mg = 0.001 g
> 1 g = 0.001 kg

Complete the following.

1. 4 kg = _____ g   4 g = _____ kg   4 g = _____ mg

2. 73 mg = _____ g   3.66 kg = _____ g   30 mg = _____ g

3. 2.6 kg = _____ g   265 g = _____ kg   40 g = _____ mg

4. 900 g = _____ kg   0.72 g = _____ mg   0.8 g = _____ kg

5. 492 g = _____ kg   6 g = _____ kg   6 g = _____ mg

6. 86,400 g = _____ kg 1.2 kg = _____ g   4 mg = _____ g

Solve each problem.

7. A nickel weighs about 5 grams. A roll of nickels contains 40 coins. How much do 8 rolls of nickels weigh?

   The nickels weigh about _____ kilograms.

8. A truck is carrying 8 crates, each weighing 55 kilograms. What is the total weight of the crates?

   The crates weigh _____ kilograms.

9. Tara needs to move three boxes. The weights of the boxes are 3.8 kilograms, 4,590 grams, and 3 kilograms. What is the total weight of the boxes?

   The boxes weigh _____ kilograms.

There are 2.2 pounds in one kilogram. Ask your child to convert his or her weight into milligrams, grams, and kilograms. One hundred kilograms would be about how many times your child's weight?

Dividing Fractions

To divide, multiply by the reciprocal of the divisor.

Example: $\frac{4}{5} \div \frac{8}{9} = \frac{4}{5} \times \frac{9}{8} = \frac{36}{40} = \frac{9}{10}$

Divide. Write answers in simplest form.

1. $\frac{1}{2} \div \frac{3}{5}$ $\frac{3}{8} \div \frac{2}{3}$ $\frac{5}{8} \div \frac{3}{4}$ $\frac{2}{5} \div \frac{3}{8}$

2. $\frac{1}{2} \div \frac{7}{8}$ $\frac{4}{5} \div \frac{3}{4}$ $\frac{5}{6} \div \frac{3}{8}$ $\frac{2}{3} \div \frac{4}{5}$

3. $\frac{7}{8} \div \frac{1}{3}$ $\frac{7}{9} \div \frac{2}{3}$ $\frac{1}{3} \div \frac{2}{3}$ $\frac{5}{6} \div \frac{1}{3}$

4. $\frac{3}{5} \div \frac{2}{3}$ $\frac{4}{9} \div \frac{3}{7}$ $\frac{1}{2} \div \frac{5}{8}$ $\frac{2}{3} \div \frac{7}{9}$

Helping at Home

Help your child understand dividing fractions by explaining that a problem like $30 \div 6$ can be stated as "How many 6s are in 30?" (5) Likewise, the problem $\frac{1}{2} \div \frac{1}{6}$ is the same as asking, "How many $\frac{1}{6}$s are in $\frac{1}{2}$?" (3)

Dividing Fractions

Examples:

$3\frac{2}{5} \div 4$ Rename $3\frac{2}{5}$ as $\frac{17}{5}$.

$\frac{17}{5} \div \frac{4}{1}$ Rename 4 as $\frac{4}{1}$.

$\frac{17}{5} \times \frac{1}{4} = \frac{17}{20}$ Multiply by the reciprocal.

$4\frac{1}{3} \div 2\frac{3}{4}$

$\frac{13}{3} \div \frac{11}{4}$ Rename.

$\frac{13}{3} \times \frac{4}{11} = \frac{52}{33} = 1\frac{19}{33}$ Multiply by the reciprocal.

Divide. Write answers in simplest form.

1. $2\frac{1}{2} \div 3\frac{1}{3}$ $1\frac{1}{8} \div 2\frac{1}{4}$ $8 \div 3\frac{1}{2}$ $2\frac{1}{3} \div 5$

2. $4\frac{1}{2} \div 1\frac{1}{6}$ $4\frac{5}{6} \div 2\frac{2}{5}$ $4\frac{1}{3} \div 6$ $1\frac{1}{2} \div 3\frac{1}{8}$

3. $6 \div 2\frac{1}{2}$ $1\frac{1}{2} \div 3$ $5 \div 3\frac{3}{4}$ $2\frac{1}{8} \div 3$

4. $3\frac{3}{5} \div 4$ $3\frac{1}{3} \div 2\frac{3}{8}$ $1 \div 4\frac{1}{3}$ $9 \div 1\frac{2}{3}$

Helping at Home   Have your child choose one problem from this page and solve it step-by-step on a large sheet of paper. Don't skip any steps! Then, have him or her explain the solution to you using the paper as a visual aid. Praise your child's careful and complete work.

Dividing Fractions

Solve each problem. Write answers in simplest form.

1. How many pieces of string that are $\frac{2}{7}$ of an inch long can be cut from a piece of string that is $\frac{7}{8}$ of an inch long?

   _____3_____ pieces of string can be cut.

2. Five pounds of walnuts will be divided equally into containers which will hold $\frac{5}{8}$ of a pound each. How many containers will be filled?

   _____8_____ containers will be filled.

3. A ribbon is $\frac{7}{9}$ of a yard long. It will be divided equally among 3 people. What is the length of ribbon that each person will get?

   Each person will get_____$\frac{7}{27}$_____ of a yard.

4. A container holding $6\frac{2}{3}$ pints of juice will be divided equally among 5 people. How much juice will each person get?

   Each person will get_____$1\frac{1}{3}$_____ pints.

5. A 7-hour class will be divided into equal sessions of $1\frac{2}{5}$ hours. How many sessions will be needed?

   _____5_____ sessions will be needed.

6. Jamie divided $6\frac{2}{5}$ ounces of candy into equal amounts. He put the candy into containers that hold $2\frac{2}{3}$ ounces each. How many containers will be filled?

   _____$2\frac{2}{5}$_____ containers will be filled.

Have your child find a food package and convert its weight to a fraction of a pound. Then, ask your child to calculate each person's portion if it were shared by the number of people in your family, the number of students in his or her class, etc.

Dividing Multi-Digit Numbers

Examples:

983 is between 840 (28 × 30) and 1120 (28 × 40), so the tens digit is 3.

```
        3
28 )9 8 3
   - 8 4 0      subtract
   ─────────
     1 4 3
```

143 is between 140 (28 × 5) and 168 (28 × 6), so the ones digit is 5.

```
        3 5r3
28 )9 8 3
   - 8 4 0        subtract
   ─────────
     1 4 3
   - 1 4 0        subtract
   ─────────
         3        remainder
```

Divide.

1. 18)9 4   27)6 8   22)8 8   19)7 8   25)6 4

2. 43)8 8   12)8 4   32)8 6 5   24)7 6 8   31)9 1 3

3. 27)8 1 5   54)7 2 5   45)8 8 0   23)6 1 5   18)3 2 4

Helping at Home

There are 365 days in a year. Have your child divide 365 by 12 (to show the number of days in a month), by 26 (to show the number of days in two weeks), and by 52 (to show the number of days in one week). What other divisors yield interesting results?

Dividing Multi-Digit Numbers

37262 is between
32800 (82 × 400) and
41000 (82 × 500), so the
hundreds digit is 4.

```
        4
82)37262
  -32800      subtract
    4462
```

4462 is between
4100 (82 × 50) and
4920 (82 × 60), so the
tens digit is 5.

```
       45
82)37262
  -32800
    4462
   -4100      subtract
     362
```

362 is between
328 (82 × 4) and
410 (82 × 5), so the
ones digit is 4.

```
      454r34
82)37262
  -32800
    4462
   -4100
     362
    -328      subtract
      34      remainder
```

Divide.

1. 56)6185   32)9984   27)3126   13)2329   22)2420

2. 45)6950   88)9944   21)5672   78)40794   65)14625

3. 36)52813   63)45675   42)34816   23)20378   18)10242

Ask your child to imagine winning a jackpot of $99,999. What would
be his or her share if 12 people won? 32 people? 85 people?

Adding Decimals

To add decimals, line up the decimal points. Then, add as you would whole numbers.

Examples:

```
  1
 26.2
+  5.3
-------
 31.5
```

```
   1
  4.65
  0.08
+ 7.34
-------
 12.07
```

```
    1
 0.086
+4.172
-------
 4.258
```

Add.

1.
```
   3.2
 + 8.5
```
```
  0.73
+ 0.88
```
```
  1.84
+ 2.39
```
```
  1.44
+ 8.37
```
```
   4.23
 +16.21
```

2.
```
 0.014
+2.301
```
```
 27.12
+13.09
```
```
 42.325
+  2.014
```
```
  6.54
+ 3.98
```
```
  0.63
+ 5.72
```

3.
```
  2.72
  3.51
+ 4.22
```
```
 68.52
  1.72
+  0.55
```
```
  27.15
 105.21
+   2.63
```
```
   7.2
   8.8
 +17.5
```
```
   0.5
   0.6
 +21.2
```

4.
```
   5.3
 + 2.8
```
```
 68.68
+  8.48
```
```
 32.132
+14.212
```
```
  76.8
 +24.3
```
```
 1.119
+2.881
```

5.
```
  6.50
 +8.72
```
```
 486.25
+103.88
```
```
 168.42
+ 35.69
```
```
 25.093
+  3.112
```
```
 14.001
+  2.883
```

6.
```
 0.113
+0.658
```
```
 4.211
+8.385
```
```
 68.682
+25.529
```
```
 2.004
+6.138
```
```
  48.6
 +53.9
```

Helping at Home

Ask your child to research prices for 10 party supplies and write them in a list, aligning the decimal points. What is the total price for all the party supplies? How much would the sales tax be for the purchase?

84

Subtracting Decimals

To subtract decimals, line up the decimal points. Then, subtract as you would whole numbers.

Examples:

$$\begin{array}{r} 25.8 \\ -11.3 \\ \hline 14.5 \end{array} \qquad \begin{array}{r} ^{3\ 1} \\ 17.\cancel{4}1 \\ -15.33 \\ \hline 2.08 \end{array} \qquad \begin{array}{r} ^{16\ \ 13\ 1} \\ \cancel{1}\cancel{7}.\cancel{4}68 \\ -\ 8.573 \\ \hline 8.895 \end{array}$$

Subtract.

1.
$$\begin{array}{r} 0.8 \\ -0.3 \\ \hline \end{array} \qquad \begin{array}{r} 2.6 \\ -1.8 \\ \hline \end{array} \qquad \begin{array}{r} 3.7 \\ -1.8 \\ \hline \end{array} \qquad \begin{array}{r} 0.96 \\ -0.27 \\ \hline \end{array} \qquad \begin{array}{r} 1.9 \\ -0.4 \\ \hline \end{array}$$

2.
$$\begin{array}{r} 18.62 \\ -11.58 \\ \hline \end{array} \qquad \begin{array}{r} 0.458 \\ -0.295 \\ \hline \end{array} \qquad \begin{array}{r} 0.867 \\ -0.532 \\ \hline \end{array} \qquad \begin{array}{r} 8.6 \\ -7.3 \\ \hline \end{array} \qquad \begin{array}{r} 11.6 \\ -\ 8.8 \\ \hline \end{array}$$

3.
$$\begin{array}{r} 43.6 \\ -27.3 \\ \hline \end{array} \qquad \begin{array}{r} 15.32 \\ -14.95 \\ \hline \end{array} \qquad \begin{array}{r} 0.65 \\ -0.32 \\ \hline \end{array} \qquad \begin{array}{r} 2.695 \\ -0.128 \\ \hline \end{array} \qquad \begin{array}{r} 8.04 \\ -0.93 \\ \hline \end{array}$$

4.
$$\begin{array}{r} 8.456 \\ -4.238 \\ \hline \end{array} \qquad \begin{array}{r} 27.8 \\ -13.4 \\ \hline \end{array} \qquad \begin{array}{r} 62.435 \\ -38.203 \\ \hline \end{array} \qquad \begin{array}{r} 14.8 \\ -\ 8.9 \\ \hline \end{array} \qquad \begin{array}{r} 12.68 \\ -\ 4.92 \\ \hline \end{array}$$

5.
$$\begin{array}{r} 19.6 \\ -\ 2.8 \\ \hline \end{array} \qquad \begin{array}{r} 18.507 \\ -\ 9.362 \\ \hline \end{array} \qquad \begin{array}{r} 54.82 \\ -28.66 \\ \hline \end{array} \qquad \begin{array}{r} 76.8 \\ -35.1 \\ \hline \end{array} \qquad \begin{array}{r} 188.4 \\ -\ 93.1 \\ \hline \end{array}$$

6.
$$\begin{array}{r} 14.72 \\ -12.86 \\ \hline \end{array} \qquad \begin{array}{r} 7.403 \\ -5.941 \\ \hline \end{array} \qquad \begin{array}{r} 4.08 \\ -1.39 \\ \hline \end{array} \qquad \begin{array}{r} 8.6 \\ -7.3 \\ \hline \end{array} \qquad \begin{array}{r} 5.8 \\ -0.9 \\ \hline \end{array}$$

Helping at Home

Have your child convert his or her height and the height of other family members to decimals. For example, 5 feet 8 inches equals 5.66 feet. What is the difference between each family member's height and a ceiling that is eight feet tall?

Multiplying Decimals

The number of digits to the right of the decimal point in the product is the sum of the number of digits to the right of the decimal point of the factors.

Examples:

```
      0.4
  ×   0.2
  ───────
     0.08
```

```
      0.28
  ×    0.6
  ─────────
     0.168
```

```
       3.2432
  ×      0.13
  ────────────
       97296
  +    32432
  ────────────
     0.421616
```

If needed, add zeros as place holders.

Multiply.

1.
```
     0.7
  ×    8
```
```
     0.08
  ×   0.5
```
```
     0.325
  ×    0.3
```
```
     1.68
  ×     8
```
```
       25
  ×  0.7
```

2.
```
     0.03
  × 3.06
```
```
     0.162
  ×    0.3
```
```
     8.03
  ×   3.5
```
```
     0.297
  ×    7.1
```
```
     76.4
  ×   3.6
```

3.
```
     53.64
  ×    0.37
```
```
     328.1
  ×    0.63
```
```
     9.806
  ×      31
```
```
     600.3
  ×   0.034
```
```
       895
  ×   0.63
```

4.
```
     27.1
  ×  3.54
```
```
     3.263
  ×      18
```
```
     1.253
  ×      12
```
```
      58.9
  ×  0.038
```
```
      0.82
  ×  0.82
```

Helping at Home

Suggest that your child use colored pencils to do several problems from this page. Use one bright color for writing zeros. Use another bright color for adding a decimal point to each answer in the correct spot.

Dividing Decimals

Multiply the divisor and dividend by 10, by 100, or by 1000 so the new divisor is a whole number.

Examples:

$$0.3\overline{)1.17} = 3\overline{)11.7}$$
Multiply by 10.

$$\begin{array}{r} 3.9 \\ 3\overline{)11.7} \\ -9 \\ \hline 27 \end{array}$$

$$0.05\overline{)7.50} = 5\overline{)750}$$
Multiply by 100.

$$\begin{array}{r} 150 \\ 5\overline{)750} \\ -5 \\ \hline 25 \\ -25 \\ \hline 0 \end{array}$$

$$0.002\overline{)3.600} = 2\overline{)3600}$$

$$\begin{array}{r} 1800 \\ 2\overline{)3600} \end{array}$$

Divide.

1. $0.8\overline{)0.168}$ $0.03\overline{)1.68}$ $0.004\overline{)0.012}$ $0.5\overline{)25.5}$

2. $0.06\overline{)2.16}$ $0.07\overline{)0.245}$ $0.009\overline{)37.8}$ $0.7\overline{)17.206}$

3. $0.3\overline{)0.027}$ $0.06\overline{)27.12}$ $0.008\overline{)4}$ $0.5\overline{)0.8}$

Helping at Home

Ask your child to choose one problem from this page to solve on a large sheet of blank paper. Use a penny or another small round object to represent a decimal point. Your child should move the decimal point around while solving the problem.

Greatest Common Factor

A **factor** is a divisor of a number. (For example, 3 and 4 are both factors of 12.) A **common factor** is a divisor that is shared by two or more numbers (1, 2, 4, and 8). The **greatest common factor** is the largest common factor shared by the numbers (8).

Example:
To find the greatest common factor of 32 and 40, list all of the factors of each.

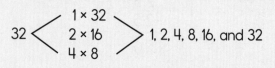

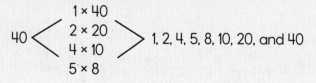

The greatest common factor is 8.

List the factors of each number below. Then, list the common factors and the greatest common factor.

	Factors	Common Factors	Greatest Common Factor
1. 8	_____	_____	_____
12	_____		
2. 6	_____	_____	_____
18	_____		
3. 24	_____	_____	_____
15	_____		
4. 4	_____	_____	_____
6	_____		
5. 5	_____	_____	_____
12	_____		
6. 16	_____	_____	_____
12	_____		

Helping at Home
Have your child compare his or her age with the ages of other family members. What is the greatest common factor for each pair of ages? Which ages are odd? Which are even? Are any of the ages prime numbers?

Least Common Multiple

The **least common multiple** (LCM) is the smallest multiple that is shared by two numbers. Rename fractions so they have common denominators by finding the LCM of the denominators.

Example:
$\frac{1}{2}$ and $\frac{2}{3}$ do not have common denominators. The LCM of 2 and 3 is 6.

$$\frac{1}{2} \times \frac{3}{3} = \frac{3}{6} \qquad\qquad \frac{2}{3} \times \frac{2}{2} = \frac{4}{6}$$

$\frac{3}{6}$ and $\frac{4}{6}$ do have common denominators.

Find the LCM and rename each pair of fractions with common denominators.

1. $\frac{1}{6}$ and $\frac{2}{5}$ _____ $\qquad$ $\frac{3}{8}$ and $\frac{1}{3}$ _____

2. $\frac{3}{4}$ and $\frac{1}{7}$ _____ $\qquad$ $\frac{1}{6}$ and $\frac{3}{4}$ _____

3. $\frac{1}{2}$ and $\frac{5}{8}$ _____ $\qquad$ $\frac{1}{4}$ and $\frac{3}{10}$ _____

4. $\frac{1}{5}$ and $\frac{4}{9}$ _____ $\qquad$ $\frac{2}{5}$ and $\frac{1}{4}$ _____

Helping at Home

You and your child each choose a number between *1 and 12*. Write as many multiples of your number as you can in 30 seconds. Then, compare lists. Circle the least common multiple. Use it as one of the numbers in the next round.

Positive and Negative Integers

Integers are the set of whole numbers and their opposites.

Positive integers are greater than zero. **Negative integers** are less than zero. Zero is neither positive nor negative. A negative integer is less than a positive integer. On a number line, an integer and its opposite are the same distance from zero. The smaller of two integers is always the one to the left on a number line.

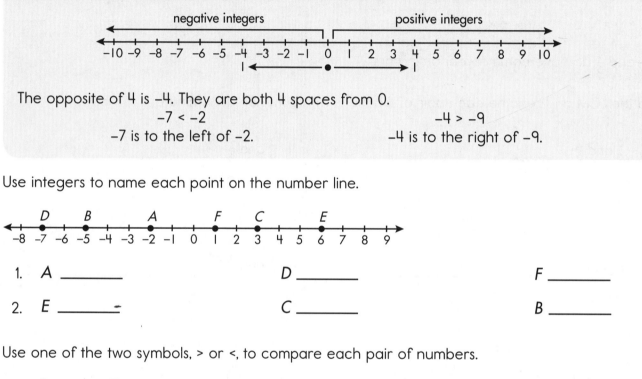

The opposite of 4 is –4. They are both 4 spaces from 0.

$-7 < -2$ $-4 > -9$

–7 is to the left of –2.   –4 is to the right of –9.

Use integers to name each point on the number line.

1. A _____   D _____   F _____

2. E _____   C _____   B _____

Use one of the two symbols, > or <, to compare each pair of numbers.

3. 2 _____ 7   –1 _____ –4   5 _____ 0

4. –4 _____ 1   0 _____ –8   –8 _____ –10

5. 7 _____ –7   –2 _____ 0   4 _____ 6

List in order from smallest to largest.

6. –3, –5, 0 _____   8, –8, 2 _____

7. 0, 5, –3, –7 _____   4, –1, 2, –2 _____

Helping at Home

Discuss the number line at the top of this page with your child. Why are the negative numbers shown to the left of zero? What does a negative number, such as –4, represent? In what ways is it similar to and different from the number 4?

Integer Problems

Solve each problem.

1. An elevator started at the first floor and went up 18 floors. It then came down 11 floors and went back up 16. At what floor was it stopped?

2. At midnight, the temperature was 30°F. By 6:00 a.m., it had dropped 5° and by noon, it had increased by 11°. What was the temperature at noon?

3. Some number added to 5 is equal to –11. Find the number.

4. From the top of a mountain to the floor of the valley below is 4,392 feet. If the valley is 93 feet below sea level, what is the height of the mountain?

5. During one week, the stock market did the following: Monday rose 18 points, Tuesday rose 31 points, Wednesday dropped 5 points, Thursday rose 27 points, and Friday dropped 38 points. If it started out at 1,196 on Monday, what did it end up on Friday?

6. An airplane started at 0 feet. It rose 21,000 feet at takeoff. It then descended 4,329 feet because of clouds. An oncoming plane was approaching, so it rose 6,333 feet. After the oncoming plane passed, it descended 8,453 feet. At what altitude was the plane flying?

© Carson-Dellosa • CD-704506

Helping at Home

Talk with your child about real-world examples of negative numbers and why they are useful. They allow us to refer to altitudes below sea level, distances underground, and negative account balances. Think of more examples together.

Plotting Ordered Pairs

In a **coordinate plane**, the axes are labeled *x* and *y*. The coordinates of a point are represented by the ordered pair (*x*, *y*). The plane is divided into four quadrants, which are named in counterclockwise order. The signs on the ordered pairs in Quadrant I are (+, +), Quadrant II are (−, +), Quadrant III are (−, −), and Quadrant IV are (+, −).

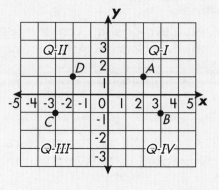

Examples:
Point *A* has the coordinates (2, 1).
Point *B* has the coordinates (3, −1).
Point *C* has the coordinates (−3, −1).
Point *D* has the coordinates (−2, 1).

Use Grid 1 to name the point for each ordered pair.

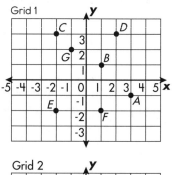

1. (2, 3) _____   (3, −1) _____

2. (−2, −2) _____   (−2, 3) _____

3. (1, −2) _____   (1, 1) _____

Use Grid 2 to find the ordered pair for each point.

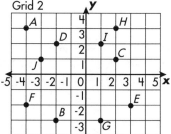

4. A _____   F _____

5. B _____   G _____

6. C _____   H _____

Plot the following points on Grid 3.

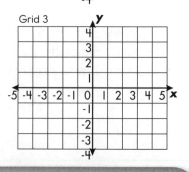

7. A (2, 3)   D (2, −3)

8. B (−1, 4)   E (3, 2)

9. C (−2, −3)   F (−4, 2)

Have your child use graph paper to create a large coordinate plane. Pin it to a bulletin board. Then, name ordered pairs such as (2, 6), (−3, 7), (5, −1), and (−8, −6). Challenge your child to insert a thumbtack at each point you name.

© Carson-Dellosa • CD-704506

Integers and Absolute Value

The sum of two positive integers is positive. The sum of two negative integers is negative.

To find the sum of two integers with different signs, find their absolute values. **Absolute value** is the distance (in units) that a number is from 0 expressed as a positive quantity. Subtract the lesser number from the greater number. Absolute value is written as $|x|$. The sum has the same sign as the integer with the larger absolute value.

Example:

To subtract an integer, add its opposite.

Example:

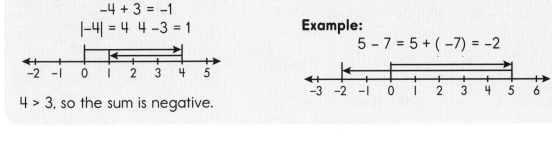

$-4 + 3 = -1$

$|-4| = 4 \quad 4 - 3 = 1$

$4 > 3$, so the sum is negative.

$5 - 7 = 5 + (-7) = -2$

Add or subtract.

1. $6 + 2 =$ _____ $9 + (-4) =$ _____ $7 + (-9) =$ _____ $-3 + 8 =$ _____

2. $3 - 11 =$ _____ $5 - 2 =$ _____ $-4 - 6 =$ _____ $8 - (-2) =$ _____

3. $-4 + 7 =$ _____ $-3 + (-6) =$ _____ $-12 + 11 =$ _____ $-16 + (-7) =$ _____

4. $-12 - 3 =$ _____ $-5 - (-6) =$ _____ $14 - 19 =$ _____ $7 - 18 =$ _____

5. $-16 + 0 =$ _____ $13 + (-24) =$ _____ $-6 + 8 =$ _____ $-3 + (-2) =$ _____

6. $4 - 19 =$ _____ $-11 - (-1) =$ _____ $16 - (-27) =$ _____ $7 - 22 =$ _____

7. $0 + (-9) =$ _____ $-1 + 2 =$ _____ $1 + (-2) =$ _____ $8 + (-8) =$ _____

8. $-6 - (-6) =$ _____ $-11 - 0 =$ _____ $-2 - 2 =$ _____ $1 - 2 =$ _____

Helping at Home

Choose a positive or negative number such as *48* or *–72*. Using positive and negative integers, absolute values, and the four operations (+, –, ×, ÷), can your child write 10 different equations to equal that number?

Order of Operations

The **order of operations** is used to find the value of an expression with more than one operation.

   1. Do all operations within parentheses.
   2. Do all multiplications and divisions in order from left to right.
   3. Do all additions and subtractions in order from left to right.

Example:

$3 \times (4 + 5) + 6 \div 3$	Do the operation inside the parentheses.
$3 \times 9 + 6 \div 3$	Multiply and divide from left to right.
$27 + 2$	Add.
29	

Name the operation that should be done first.

1. $7 \times 3 + 2$ _____ $2 + 3 \times 5$ _____ $4 + 3 - 5$ _____

2. $8 - 6 + 4$ _____ $7 + 9 \div 3$ _____ $12 \div 3 \times 5$ _____

3. $(3 + 5) \times (3 + 1)$ _____ $(5 - 3) \div 2$ _____ $(2 + 5) \times 3$ _____

Find the value of each expression.

4. $5 \times (5 - 3)$ _____ $5 + 4 \times 3 + 6$ _____

5. $20 - 4 \times 3$ _____ $(32 \div 8) \times 2$ _____

6. $15 \div 3 + 16 \div 4$ _____ $4 \times 3 \div 6 - 1$ _____

7. $20 \div 5 \times 2$ _____ $(7 \times 8) - (4 \times 9)$ _____

8. $6 \times 5 - 5 \times 4$ _____ $84 \div (8 + 6) \div 3$ _____

9. $(7 - 3) \times 2$ _____ $16 \div (8 - 6)$ _____

10. $(2 \times 5) \times 4$ _____ $2 \times (5 \times 4)$ _____

Helping at Home

Write a series of numbers such as *48, 2, 12, 8, 6, 10* three times in three rows on a large sheet of paper. Can your child add operations symbols (+, −, x, ÷) and parentheses to form three different equations with three different solutions?

Exponents

A number multiplied by itself can be written as follows: $2 \times 2 \times 2 \times 2 = 2^4 = 16$. In the expression 2^4, the small superscript 4 is called the **exponent**, and the 2 is called the **base**. An exponent is a number that indicates repeated multiplication. It shows how many times to multiply the base, the number that is being multiplied by itself.

A number raised to the first power (n^1) is simply itself. For example, $2^1 = 2$.

A number, other than 0, raised to the 0 power (n^0) is 1. For example, $2^0 = 1$.

When solving equations with exponents, keep in mind that the Distributive Property does not apply to exponents outside parentheses. For example, $(2 + 5)^2 = (2 + 5)(2 + 5) = 7 \times 7 = 49$. It does not equal $2^2 + 5^2$ (which is 4 + 25, or 29).

Rewrite each of the following using a base and exponent.

1. $5 \times 5 \times 5 =$ _____ $(3)(3)(3)(3)(3)(3) =$ _____ $b \times b \times b \times b =$ _____

2. $23 \times 1 =$ _____ $n \times n \times n \times n \times n =$ _____ $12 \times 12 =$ _____

Rewrite each of the following without a base and exponent.

3. $3^3 =$ _____ $11^2 =$ _____ $13^0 =$ _____

4. $5^4 =$ _____ $10^5 =$ _____ $55^1 =$ _____

Solve the following equations.

5. $3^2 + 2^3 =$ _____ $(4 + 2)^2 =$ _____ $(5 - 1)^3 =$ _____ $3^3 - 5^2 =$ _____

6. $3^4 + 6 =$ _____ $(3 + 1)^3 =$ _____ $2^5 - 10 =$ _____ $n + 7^2 = 50$ _____

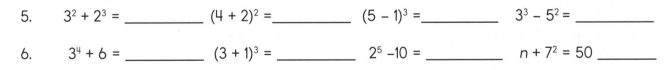

Helping at Home

Have your child research a favorite topic such as outer space or soccer and find a very large related number. For example, Mars is 35 million miles from Earth. Can your child express the number by writing 100 or 1000 plus an exponent?

Understanding Expressions and Equations

A **variable** is a symbol, usually a letter of the alphabet, that stands for an unknown number or quantity. **Example:** a = variable

An **algebraic expression** is a combination of numbers, variables, and at least one operation. **Example:** $x + 13$

A **term** is a number, variable, product, or quotient in an algebraic expression. **Example:** In $3a + 5$, $3a$ is a term and 5 is also a term. The term $3a$ means $3 \times a$. The number 3 is the coefficient of a.

A **coefficient** is a number that multiplies a variable. **Example:** In the expression $x + 5$, the coefficient of x is understood to be 1.

An **equation** is a sentence that contains an equal sign. **Example:** $x + 13 = 25$

Identify each of the following as an expression or an equation.

1. $3 + x$ _____ $7 + 4 = 11$ _____ $55 \times n$ _____

For each term below, identify the coefficient and the variable.

2. $3x$ coefficient _____ variable _____ $4y$ coefficient _____ variable _____

Translate each phrase into an algebraic expression.

3. five more than n _____   eight decreased by x _____

4. x added to seven _____   the product of n and 11 _____

Translate each sentence into an equation.

5. Six times a number is 18. _____   Seventy less a number is 29. _____

6. Eight divided by a number is 2. _____   The product of 7 and 12 is 84. _____

Write the following expressions in words.

7. $6 - n = 3$ _____

8. $5 \times 13 = 65$ _____

Helping at Home

Talk with your child about the definition of *algebra*. It is the part of mathematics that uses letters and symbols to represent numbers in equations. It allows us to find unknown quantities. Show excitement that your child is beginning to study algebra.

Writing Expressions

The product of four and eleven	$4 \cdot 11$
A number increased by six	$x + 6$
The number divided by two	$y \div 2$ or $\dfrac{y}{2}$
Twice a number decreased by one	$2a - 1$

Write the expressions.

1. Five less than a number

2. Three times the sum of a number and twelve

3. Ten more than the quotient of c and three

4. Two increased by six times a number

5. Two-thirds of a number minus eleven

6. Twice the difference between c and four

7. The product of nine and a number, decreased by seven

8. Six times a number plus seven times the number

9. A number increased by twice the number

10. One-fourth times a number increased by eleven

Helping at Home

Encourage your child to ask math-related questions about everyday situations. He or she might ask, "How many more games did our team play in April than in March?" Challenge your child to write an algebraic expression to state the problem.

Evaluating Expressions

$$5x\,(2a - 5y) = 5 \bullet 4\,\left(2 \bullet \frac{1}{2} - 5 \bullet {}^-2\right) = 20\,(1 + 10) = 20\,(11) = 220$$

Evaluate the following, if $a = \dfrac{1}{2}$, $x = 4$, and $y = {}^-2$.

1. $4\,(a - 1) =$

2. $4a - 3y =$

3. $4\,(x - 3y) =$

4. $x\,(a + 6) =$

5. $6a + {}^-12a =$

6. $7\,(x + -y) =$

7. $6a\,(8a + 4y) =$

8. $3x + 2\,(a - y) =$

9. $x\,(ax + ay) =$

10. $ay + y - 5ax =$

11. $xy\,(2a + 3x - 2) =$

12. $4x - (xy + 2) =$

13. $5y - 8a + 6xy - 7x =$

14. $10x\,(8a + {}^-4y) + {}^-3y =$

15. $6xy - 2x\,(4a - 8y) =$

16. $(2a - x)\,(2x - 6) =$

Helping at Home

Come up with different values for the variables a, x, and y. Challenge your child to evaluate several expressions on this page using those values.

The Distributive Property

The **distributive property** combines the operations of addition and multiplication.

Example: $a \times (b + c)$ = $(a \times b) + (a \times c)$
              $3 \times (2 + 5)$ $(3 \times 2) + (3 \times 5)$
              3×7 $6 + 15$
              21 21

Indicate which operation should be done first.

1. $(2 \times 5) + (2 \times 3)$ _____ $7 \times (3 + 5)$ _____

2. $(6 + 9) \times 4$ _____ $(3 \times 5) + (3 \times 7)$ _____

Rewrite each expression using the distributive property.

3. $4 \times (6 + 2) =$ _____ $(2 \times 5) + (2 \times 4) =$ _____

4. $(5 \times 1) + (5 \times 6) =$ _____ $4 \times (2 + 6) =$ _____

Write each missing number.

5. $(5 \times 3) + (n \times 4) = 5 \times (3 + 4)$ _____ $7 \times (n + 3) = (7 \times 2) + (7 \times 3)$ _____

6. $n \times (5 + 3) = (6 \times 5) + (6 \times 3)$ _____ $(5 \times 7) + (n \times 4) = 5 \times (7 + 4)$ _____

Replace a with 2, b with 5, and c with 3. Then, find the value of each expression.

7. $a \times (b + c) =$ _____ $(a \times b) + (a \times c) =$ _____

8. $(c \times a) + (c \times b) =$ _____ $b \times (a + c) =$ _____

Helping at Home

Discuss the distributive property with your child. Explain that, for the expression 3 x (2 + 4), the distributive property means that three groups of 2 + 4 is the same as three groups of two plus three groups of 4. Can your child make a visual model?

Simplifying Expressions

Distributive Property

$3(x + 2y) = 3x + 3 \cdot 2y$
$= 3x + 6y$

1. $-7(a + b) =$

2. $x(y - 4) =$

3. $-\dfrac{2}{3}(c - 12) =$

4. $-8\left(\dfrac{t}{2} + 6\right) =$

5. $y(-16 + 2x) =$

6. $3(2a - 8b) =$

7. $2x(3y + {}^{-}6) =$

8. $7({}^{-}5x + 8z) =$

9. $-5y(6z - 10) =$

10. $-3x({}^{-}7 + 8y) =$

Combining Like Terms

$6m - 4m + 3p = (6 - 4)m + 3p$
$= 2m + 3p$
same variable

1. $9y + 6y - 2 =$

2. $25x - x + 2y =$

3. $4a + 8b + 11a - 10b =$

4. $13xy + 18xy - 20xy =$

5. $-2m + 16 - 13m =$

6. $4a + 7 + 3a - 8 - 3a =$

7. $16x + {}^{-}18y + 10x - 7y =$

8. $6c - 8ab + 9c - 10 =$

9. $18ab + {}^{-}6a + {}^{-}7b + 26ab + {}^{-}7b =$

10. $5x - 3x + 2xy + 31x + {}^{-}18xy =$

Helping at Home

Help your child think aloud as he or she solves several problems on this page. For item #2 in the second group, your child might explain, "The first two terms have the same variable, x, so they can be combined. The third term has a different variable, y."

Solving Addition and Subtraction Equations

Subtraction Property of Equality
If you subtract the same number from each side of an equation, the two sides remain equal.

Example:
$$x + 12 = 20$$
To undo the addition of 12, subtract 12.
$$x + 12 - 12 = 20 - 12$$
$$x + 0 = 8$$
$$x = 8$$

Addition Property of Equality
If you add the same number to each side of an equation, the two sides remain equal.

Example:
$$n - 3 = 15$$
To undo the subtraction of 3, add 3.
$$n - 3 + 3 = 15 + 3$$
$$n - 0 = 12$$
$$n = 12$$

Write the operation that would undo the operation in the equation.

1. $x - 4 = 3$ _____

2. $y + 7 = 25$ _____

$8 = b + 4$ _____

$3 = a - 7$ _____

Solve each equation.

3. $a - 4 = 2$ _____

4. $7 = x - 4$ _____

5. $z - 7 = 5$ _____

6. $x + 7 = 10$ _____

7. $b + 4 = 4$ _____

8. $z - 10 = 20$ _____

$y + 5 = 9$ _____

$b + 7 = 19$ _____

$m - 5 = 5$ _____

$x - 3 = 18$ _____

$b - 8 = 12$ _____

$z + 5 = 20$ _____

$x - 3 = 14$ _____

$y + 5 = 5$ _____

$n + 1 = 1$ _____

$x + 0 = 9$ _____

$n + 8 = 12$ _____

$x - 2 = 8$ _____

Write and solve the equation for each problem below.

9. Kelley went to the movies. She took 20 dollars with her. When she came home, she had 6 dollars. How much money did she spend? _____

10. There are 27 students in Mrs. Yuen's homeroom. Twelve of them have home computers. How many students do not have home computers? _____

Helping at Home
When solving equations, encourage your child to think of the equal sign as the fulcrum of a balance scale. In order to solve the equation and keep it in balance, operations (addition and subtraction) must be used equally on each side.

Solving Multiplication and Division Equations

Division Property of Equality
If you divide each side of an equation by the same nonzero number, the two sides remain equal.

Example:
$$3 \times y = 21$$
To undo multiplication by 3, divide by 3.
$$\frac{3 \times y}{3} = \frac{21}{3}$$
$$y = 7$$

Multiplication Property of Equality
If you multiply each side of an equation by the same number, the two sides remain equal.

Example:
$$\frac{a}{4} = 5$$
To undo division by 4, multiply by 4.
$$\frac{a}{4} \times \frac{4}{1} = 5 \times 4$$
$$a = 20$$

Write the operation that would undo the operation in each equation.

1. $5 \times n = 40$ _____

2. $\frac{x}{2} = 8$ _____

$\frac{y}{5} = 80$ _____

$a \times 7 = 42$ _____

Solve each equation.

3. $3 \times a = 9$ _____

4. $\frac{x}{3} = 3$ _____

5. $5 \times b = 10$ _____

6. $\frac{m}{3} = 1$ _____

7. $4 \times n = 1$ _____

8. $n \times 15 = 30$ _____

9. $\frac{n}{18} = 2$ _____

10. $\frac{n}{2} = 20$ _____

$\frac{x}{5} = 5$ _____

$n \times 4 = 4$ _____

$\frac{b}{8} = 2$ _____

$8 \times n = 20$ _____

$\frac{n}{4} = 5$ _____

$\frac{n}{4} = 10$ _____

$n \times 3 = 18$ _____

$\frac{n}{16} = 1$ _____

$\frac{n}{4} = 3$ _____

$3 \times y = 24$ _____

$4 \times a = 20$ _____

$\frac{x}{5} = 2$ _____

$\frac{b}{3} = 27$ _____

$n \times 12 = 36$ _____

$n \times 2 = 20$ _____

$n \times 3 = 3$ _____

Helping at Home

Have your child choose one equation from this page. Challenge your child to multiply and divide the terms on each side of the equation several times using different numbers. Do the two sides remain equal?

Inequalities

Recall that the = symbol means *equal to*. This symbol indicates an equation, or equality. An **inequality** states that values are not equal. The symbols > and < indicate inequality. Sometimes the values in an inequality might also be equal. For example, a tank holds 15 gallons of gas. How much gas is in the tank? You don't know without measuring. However, you do know that the amount must be less than or equal to 15 gallons: Gas in tank ≤ 15 gallons.

Symbol	Meaning
>	greater than
<	less than
≥	greater than or equal to
≤	less than or equal to

You can use inequality symbols to compare percents, fractions, and decimals. First, express the numbers in the same format so they are easier to compare.

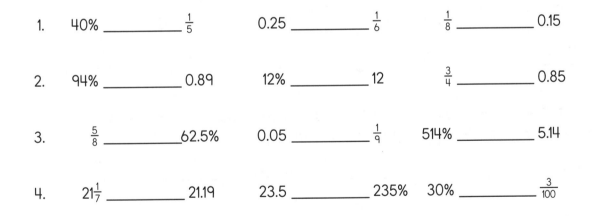

$\frac{1}{5}$ _____ 30%   0.45 _____ 38%

20% _____ 30%   Convert 1 of the numbers.   45% _____ 38%

20% ___<___ 30%   Compare the numbers.   45% ___>___ 38%

Write >, <, or = on the line to compare the given values.

1. 40% _____ $\frac{1}{5}$ 0.25 _____ $\frac{1}{6}$ $\frac{1}{8}$ _____ 0.15

2. 94% _____ 0.89   12% _____ 12 $\frac{3}{4}$ _____ 0.85

3. $\frac{5}{8}$ _____ 62.5%   0.05 _____ $\frac{1}{9}$ 514% _____ 5.14

4. $21\frac{1}{7}$ _____ 21.19   23.5 _____ 235%   30% _____ $\frac{3}{100}$

Solving Inequalities

The Addition and Subtraction Properties also apply to inequalities. You can add or subtract the same number from both sides of an inequality without affecting the inequality.

Solve: $n + 4 < 9$ $n + 4 - 4 < 9 - 4$ $n < 5$

The solution is that n can be any value less than 5.

If you swap the left side and right side of an inequality, you must reverse the direction of the inequality. The direction is the way the arrow points.

$n < 5$	$x - 6 > 3$	$p \leq 9$	$k - 7 \geq 6$
$5 > n$	$3 < x - 6$	$9 \geq p$	$6 \leq k - 7$
< becomes >	> becomes <	≤ becomes ≥	≥ becomes ≤

Solve each inequality. Show the solution with the variable on the left side.

1. $x + 5 > 8$ _____ $t - 4 < 11$ _____ $12 < m + 6$ _____

2. $y - 3 \leq 7$ _____ $9 + r \geq 5$ _____ $15 \geq 7 + n$ _____

3. $p + 1 < -5$ _____ $z + 3 + 5 < 28$ _____ $-4 \leq w + 12$ _____

4. $x - 6 \geq 8$ _____ $p + 4 \leq 35$ _____ $22 \geq y + 5 - 7$ _____

5. Jermaine has $25. He wants to buy a pair of gloves that costs $16.50. He also wants to buy a sandwich. How much can Jermaine spend on the sandwich?

Inequality: _____ Solution: _____

Helping at Home

Write a simple inequality such as *.65 < 3/4* . Ask your child to add or subtract a variety of numbers, performing the same operation on each side. Is the inequality still true?

Solving Inequalities

Multiplication and Division Properties also apply to inequalities. You can multiply or divide both sides of an inequality by the same positive number without affecting the inequality. But if you multiply or divide both sides by a negative number, you must reverse the direction of the inequality.

Solve: $4x > 12$	Solve: $\frac{n}{2} \le 8$	Solve: $-3p < 6$
$\frac{4x}{4} > \frac{12}{4}$	$\frac{n}{2} \times 2 \le 8 \times 2$	$\frac{-3p}{-3} > \frac{-6}{-3}$ reverse the inequality
$x > 3$	$n \le 16$	$p > -2$

Remember to reverse the direction of the inequality if you swap the left and the right sides.

Solve each inequality. Show the solution with the variable on the left side.

1. $5y < 15$ _____ $\frac{k}{6} > 7$ _____ $12 \le 4n$ _____

2. $-7h > 28$ _____ $\frac{m}{-4} < 5$ _____ $\frac{c}{6} \ge -2$ _____

3. $-9p > -18$ _____ $9 \le \frac{n}{3}$ _____ $30 < 3a$ _____

4. $4 < -4n$ _____ $2 \le \frac{b}{-3}$ _____ $2.5x > 40$ _____

5. Kevin has \$26 and wants to rent a bicycle. The bicycle rents for \$6.25 per hour. How many hours can Kevin ride without owing more money than he has?

   Inequality: _____ Solution: _____

Helping at Home
Ask your child to choose three inequalities from the page and swap the left and right terms. Can he or she change the signs accordingly? Talk about the meaning of the signs ≥ and ≤. They mean "greater than or equal to" and "less than or equal to."

Finding Area

The **area** of a rectangle is the number of square units inside that rectangle. Area is expressed in **square units** or **units²**.

The area of a rectangle is the product of its length and its width.

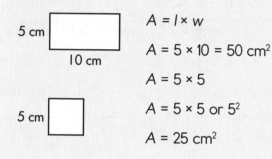

$A = l \times w$

$A = 5 \times 10 = 50 \text{ cm}^2$

$A = 5 \times 5$

$A = 5 \times 5 \text{ or } 5^2$

$A = 25 \text{ cm}^2$

If you know the area of a rectangle and either its length or its width, you can determine the unknown measure.

$A = 24 \text{ m}^2$

6 m

$A = l \times w$

$24 = 6 \times w$

$\frac{24}{6} = \frac{6w}{6}$

$4 = w$

The width is 4 meters.

Find the unknown measure for each rectangle below.

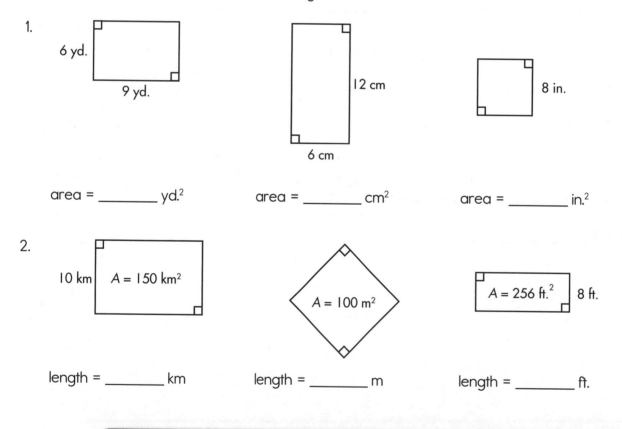

1.

6 yd.

9 yd.

12 cm

6 cm

8 in.

area = _____ yd.²

area = _____ cm²

area = _____ in.²

2.

10 km   A = 150 km²

A = 100 m²

A = 256 ft.²   8 ft.

length = _____ km

length = _____ m

length = _____ ft.

Helping at Home

Ask your child to measure one or more rooms in your home and calculate the area in square feet. Then, research the square foot price of carpet or another floor covering. How much would it cost to install new flooring in the room?

Finding Area

The **area** of a triangle equals $\frac{1}{2}$ the base times the height.

$$A = \frac{1}{2} \times b \times h$$

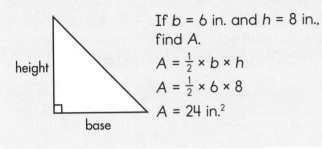

If b = 6 in. and h = 8 in., find A.

$A = \frac{1}{2} \times b \times h$

$A = \frac{1}{2} \times 6 \times 8$

$A = 24$ in.^{2}

The height is the distance from the base to the highest point on the triangle, using a line perpendicular to the base.

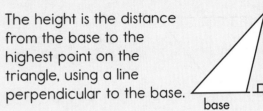

Find the area of each triangle below.

1.

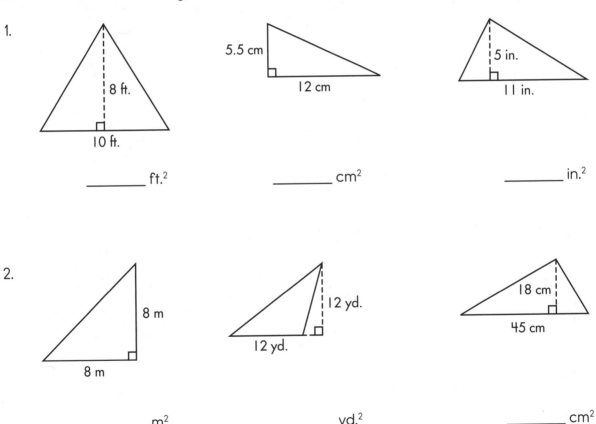

8 ft.

10 ft.

_____ ft.^{2}

5.5 cm

12 cm

_____ cm^2

5 in.

11 in.

_____ in.^{2}

2.

8 m

8 m

_____ m^2

12 yd.

12 yd.

_____ yd.^{2}

18 cm

45 cm

_____ cm^2

Helping at Home

A pyramid has four faces that are triangles. Ask your child to research the dimensions of a famous pyramid in Egypt. Can he or she calculate the area of each face? Be sure to keep units consistent.

Finding Area

A parallelogram is a polygon with 2 sets of parallel sides. To find the **area** of a parallelogram, multiply the measure of its base by the measure of its height: $A = b \times h$ or $A = bh$.

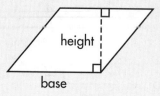

If $b = 8$ in. and $h = 7$ in., what is A?
$A = b \times h$ $A = 8 \times 7 = 56$ in.^{2}, or 56 square inches.

Find the area of each parallelogram below.

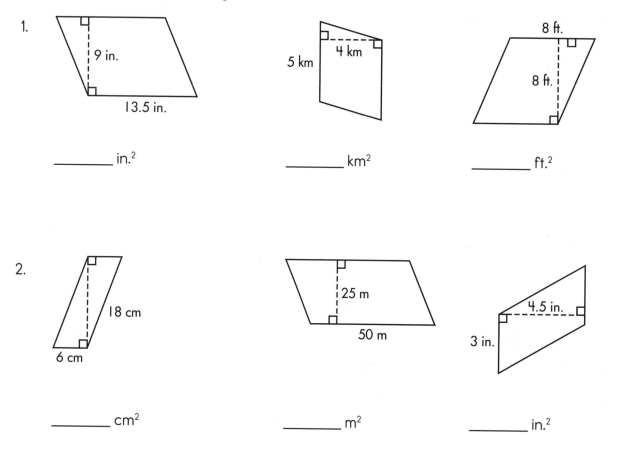

1.

9 in.

13.5 in.

_____ in.^{2}

4 km

5 km

_____ km^2

8 ft.

8 ft.

_____ ft.^{2}

2.

18 cm

6 cm

_____ cm^2

25 m

50 m

_____ m^2

4.5 in.

3 in.

_____ in.^{2}

Helping at Home

Squares, rectangles, and rhombuses (diamonds) are all parallelograms. Choose an area, such as 36 square inches. Can your child draw a square, rectangle, rhombus, and standard parallelogram (as shown on this page) with that same area?

Finding Area

To find the **area** of irregular shapes, separate the shapes into figures for which you can find the area.

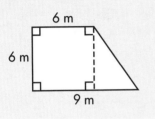

6 m

6 m

9 m

This irregular shape can be divided into a square and a triangle.

Area of square:
$A = 6 \times 6 = 36$

Area of triangle:
$A = \frac{1}{2} \times 3 \times 6 = 9$

The area of the irregular shape is $36 + 9 = 45$ square meters.

Find the area of each irregular shape below.

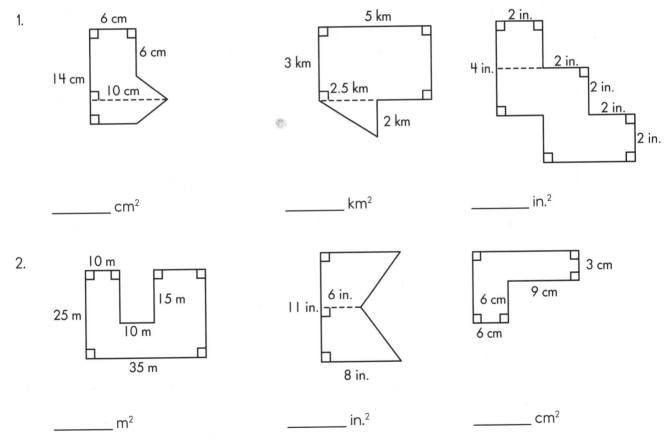

1.

6 cm

6 cm

14 cm

10 cm

_____ cm²

5 km

3 km

2.5 km

2 km

_____ km²

2 in.

4 in.

2 in.

2 in.

2 in.

2 in.

_____ in.²

2.

10 m

15 m

25 m

10 m

35 m

_____ m²

6 in.

11 in.

8 in.

_____ in.²

3 cm

6 cm

9 cm

6 cm

_____ cm²

Helping at Home

Have your child measure or research the dimensions of an irregularly shaped yard or park. Using a satellite map found on the Internet may help. Can your child calculate the area of the space in square yards?

Finding Volume

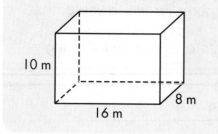

Example:
Volume = length (ℓ) × width (w) × height (h)
Volume = (16 × 8 × 10) cubic m
Volume = 1280 cubic m

Find the volume of each rectangular solid.

1.

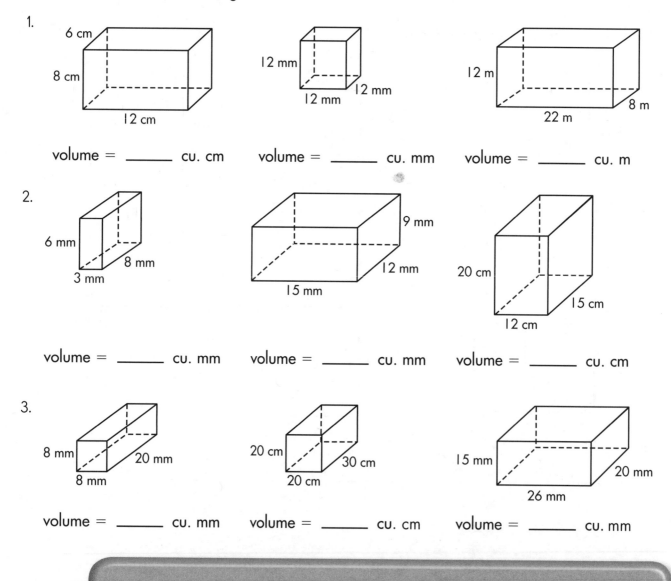

volume = _____ cu. cm   volume = _____ cu. mm   volume = _____ cu. m

2.

volume = _____ cu. mm   volume = _____ cu. mm   volume = _____ cu. cm

3.

volume = _____ cu. mm   volume = _____ cu. cm   volume = _____ cu. mm

Ask your child to imagine designing a swimming pool for your yard or neighborhood. What could the dimensions of the pool be to fit the available space? What volume of water would the pool hold?

Using Nets to Find Surface Area

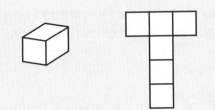 A **net** is a pattern that can be folded to cover a solid figure. The area of the net equals the surface area of the solid.

Match the net with its solid and find the the surface area. (Assume each square is 1 cm².)

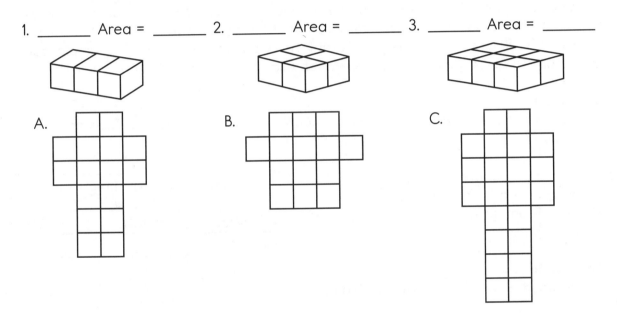

1. _____ Area = _____ 2. _____ Area = _____ 3. _____ Area = _____

A.

B.

C.

4. On the grid, draw a net for the rectangular prism shown and calculate its surface area.

Prism   Net   Area _____

 Helping at Home Have your child use a ruler and pencil to fill a blank sheet of paper with one-inch squares. Then, ask him or her to cut on some of the lines to form a net. What three-dimensional shapes can be formed from the net?

Collecting Data

Step 1: Ask a question

What do you want to learn from your study? Be specific! For example, you might want to know which brand of tomato soup is most nutritious. Your question might be: Which brand of tomato soup provides the most protein with the least fat?

Step 2: Identify your sample

Identify the population you want to study. A **population** is the set of all items of interest to your study. A population might be all brands of tomato soup offered for sale in your town.

You probably cannot collect data from every member of the population. Instead, you can collect data from a **sample**, or part of the population. The sample must accurately represent the whole population. You want to be able to draw conclusions about the population based on the sample. A sample is **biased** if it does not accurately represent the population. In the soup example, our sample might be all brands of tomato soup offered for sale at three stores in your community.

Step 3: Collect data

First, identify the data you want to collect. **Data** are items of information, such as facts or statistics. In our study, we want data on protein and fat.

Next, decide how to collect the data. To gather data about soup, you might go to three stores. You would record all brands of tomato soup and the amounts of protein and fat in each.

Nutrition Facts about Tomato Soup in grams (g)		
Brand	**Protein**	**Total Fat**
X	5 g	2 g
Y	6 g	4 g
Z	2 g	1 g

Step 4: Analyze data

Organize your data in a meaningful way, such as in a table.

How can you analyze this data to determine the answer to your question: Which brand provides the most protein with the least fat? One way is to use fractions to find the total fat per gram of protein in each brand. Then, convert the factions to decimals to make them easier to compare.

Brand X: 2 g fat/5 g protein = 0.4 g fat per gram of protein
Brand Y: 4 g fat/6 g protein = 0.7 g fat per gram of protein (rounded)
Brand Z: 1 g fat/2 g protein = 0.5 g fat per gram of protein

Step 5: Interpret results

From your analysis, you could conclude that Brand X is the most nutritious soup, because it contains the least fat per gram of protein.

Collecting Data

Now, design your own study.

Step 1: Ask a question. What is the most popular _____ among males and females? You fill in the blank. For example, you might fill in *pet, color,* or *sport.*

Step 2: Identify your sample. Choose a sample of 20 people, 10 males and 10 females. You can include family, friends, and classmates.

Step 3: Collect data. List 4 choices within the category you chose. For example, if your category is *pet,* you might list *cat, dog, snake,* and *bird.* Design a survey form that lists the choices and asks people to rank them from 1 (least favorite) to 4 (most favorite). Include a way for people to identify themselves as male or female. Collect the completed forms.

Step 4: Analyze data. List your 4 choices in the first column of the table below. Divide the surveys into those submitted by males and those submitted by females. Add the scores for the first choice from all males. Write this total in the first cell below *Males.* Add the scores for the second choice from all males. Write this total in the second cell under *Males.* After you complete the column for males, add scores for the *Females* column. Complete the *Total Score* column by totaling the scores across rows.

Which choice received the highest total score?

_____

What fraction of this total score came from males?

_____

What fraction of this total score came from females?

_____

Popularity of _____			
Choices	**Males**	**Females**	**Total Score**

Step 5: Interpret results. Write a one-sentence answer to your study question.

_____

_____

Suggest that your child make several different graphs to represent the results of his or her study. They could include a pie chart, bar graph, or line graph. Your child may wish to use a spreadsheet program or online app for help in making the graphs.

Measures of Central Tendency

The **mean** is the average of a set of numbers. To find the mean, add all the numbers and divide by the number of addends.

The **median** is the middle number of a set of numbers. If there are two middle numbers, the median is the average of the two.

The **mode** is the number that appears most often in a set of numbers.

The **range** is the difference between the greatest and the least number of the set.

Example: 12, 15, 18, 23, 8, 10, and 12
Mean: 12 + 15 + 18 + 23 + 8 + 10 + 12 = 98 $\frac{98}{7}$ = 14
Median: Arrange the numbers in order: 8, 10, 12, 12, 15, 18, 23. The median is 12.
Mode: 12
Range: 23 – 8 = 15

Find the mean, median, mode, and range of each set of numbers. Show your work.

1. 32, 35, 25, 43, 43

    mean _____

    median _____

    mode _____

    range _____

    8, 12, 23, 12, 15

    mean _____

    median _____

    mode _____

    range _____

2. 52, 61, 79, 78, 56, 79, 71

    mean _____

    median _____

    mode _____

    range _____

    37, 50, 67, 83, 34, 49, 37

    mean _____

    median _____

    mode _____

    range _____

Helping at Home

Have your child collect a set of numbers that is meaningful to him or her. The numbers could be classroom grades, sports scores, or amounts of money saved. Ask your child to calculate the mean, median, mode, and range of the numbers.

Measures of Central Tendency

Another way to examine a set of data is to look at how spread out the data is. Range is a measure of spread. The **range** of a set of numbers is the difference between the greatest and least numbers in the set.

Find the mean and range of these sets of data.

Set A: 60, 64, 59, 57, 60

order the numbers: 57, 59, 60, 60, 64

range: 64 − 57 = 7

mean: $\frac{300}{5}$ = 60

Set B: 52, 35, 75, 110, 28

order the numbers: 28, 35, 52, 75, 110

range: 110 − 28 = 82

mean: $\frac{300}{5}$ = 60

Both sets of data have a mean of 60. However, Set B has a larger range than Set A. The larger range means that the data are more spread out in Set B than in Set A.

The following table lists test scores for 3 students. Use the table to answer the questions.

Student	Test 1	Test 2	Test 3	Test 4	Test 5
Cory	88	93	81	97	84
Kara	85	84	84	86	83
Suki	90	92	88	85	92

1. Write Cory's scores in order: _____

   Cory's mean: _____   median: _____   mode: _____   range: _____

2. Write Kara's scores in order: _____

   Kara's mean: _____   median: _____   mode: _____   range: _____

3. Write Suki's scores in order: _____

   Suki's mean: _____   median: _____   mode: _____   range: _____

4. Which student performed most consistently on the tests? Explain how you know.

   _____

Helping at Home

What is the range of the heights of your child's family members and friends? Encourage your child to measure the heights of at least 10 people, record the data, and calculate the range.

Measures of Central Tendency

Each measure of central tendency provides a useful, but different, way to analyze sets of data. The mean evens out, or balances, a set of data. The mean is a good way to describe the middle of a set of data that does not have an outlier. An **outlier** is an extreme value, a number that is much larger or smaller than the other numbers in the set.

The median is a good way to describe the middle of a set that does have an outlier. An outlier affects the median less than the mean. The mode is useful for data that are not numbers. For example, you might use the mode to identify the most popular item in a set.

Consider this ordered set: 9, 9, 10, 10, 14, 35   mean = 87 ÷ 6 = 14.5   median = 10

The number 35 is much higher than the other numbers. What if we remove the outlier?

Set with outlier removed: 9, 9, 10, 10, 14   mean = 52 ÷ 5 = 10.4   median = 10

Without the outlier, the mean declined significantly, but the median was not affected.

The hourly wages of employees at two stores are shown below. Use measures of central tendency to analyze the data. Round to the nearest cent.

	Sam's Pet World	Beth's Pets
Hourly wages ($)	10, 9.5, 8.25, 9, 10, 9.5, 8.5, 10.5	9.25, 8, 7.5, 8.5, 7.75, 20, 8, 9
1. mean	$_____	$_____
2. median	$_____	$_____
3. mode	$_____	$_____

4. Which store do you think pays its employees better? Explain your answer.

_____

_____

Helping at Home

Encourage your child to research prices for a new jacket, music player, bike, or other item. Find at least eight different prices for similar items. Calculate the mean, median, and mode. Are any of the prices outliers? If so, omit and recalculate.

Dot Plots

A **dot plot** is a graph that shows frequency of data on a number line. Dot plots make it easy to identify the mode, range, and any outliers. Recall that an outlier is an extreme value, a number that is much larger or smaller than the other numbers in the set.

To make a dot plot, draw a number line from the least to the greatest value in the number set. Then, make an **X** above each number every time it appears in the set. The number of Xs above each number shows how many times that number appears—its frequency.

Height of My Classmates

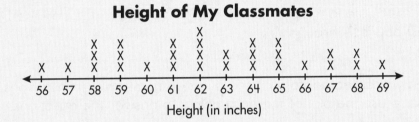

Height (in inches)

What is the mode, or most frequent height? Look for the tallest stack of Xs. The mode is 62 inches. What is the range of heights in the class? Subtract the least height from the greatest: 69 – 56 = 13 inches. How many students were polled? Count the total number of Xs. Thirty students were polled. What is the median height of the students? Count 15 Xs in from the left and 15 Xs in from the right. The median is the average of these two numbers. Because both numbers are 62 inches, the median is 62 inches.

The Eagles baseball team scored these numbers of runs per game: 4, 2, 6, 3, 1, 0, 2, 0, 4, 5, 0, 7, 6, 4, 3, 2, 6, 8, 1, 3, 11, 7, 3. Make a dot plot. Then, answer the questions.

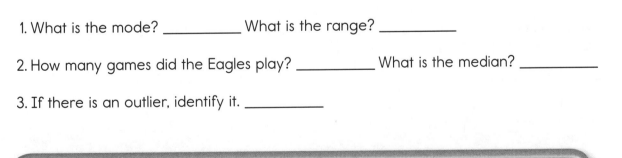

1. What is the mode? _____ What is the range? _____

2. How many games did the Eagles play? _____ What is the median? _____

3. If there is an outlier, identify it. _____

Helping at Home

Encourage your child to count items in his or her room such as books, pairs of socks, posters, and pillows. Make a dot plot to show the counts of each item. Then, ask your child to write three questions for you to answer based on the completed dot plot.

Dot Plots

Dot plots can also help you see clusters and gaps in the data. **Clusters** are groups of points separated from other points. **Gaps** are large spaces between points.

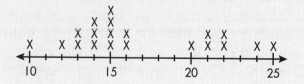

The largest clusters of data in the plot lie in the 12 through 16 range and the 20 through 22 range. The largest gap is 17 through 19.

As a store manager, you collected data on the average number of transactions that each sales clerk handled in a day. Use the plot of the data below to answer the questions.

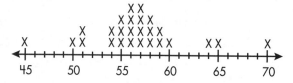

1. What is the mode? _____

2. What is the data range? _____

3. How many sales clerks does the store employ? _____

4. What is the median number of transactions? _____

5. Based on the data, what range of transactions would you consider a standard day's work for a sales clerk? Explain why.

   _____

6. Above what number of transactions would you consider giving an award for employee of the month? Explain your reasoning.

   _____

Helping at Home

Brainstorm different possible data sets with your child. You may consider the number of leaves on trees at different times of the year or the age at which children lose their first tooth. What might be the overall shape of a dot plot in each instance?

Histograms

A **histogram** is a type of bar graph. In a histogram, the categories are consecutive and the intervals are equal. Each bar shows a range of data. There is no space between the bars.

A histogram is created from a **frequency table**, as shown below.
An interval that does not have a frequency does not have a bar.

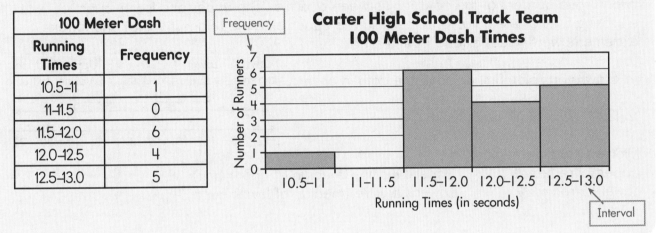

100 Meter Dash	
Running Times	**Frequency**
10.5–11	1
11–11.5	0
11.5–12.0	6
12.0–12.5	4
12.5–13.0	5

**Carter High School Track Team
100 Meter Dash Times**

Refer to the table and histogram above to answer the following questions.

1. Which interval has the greatest number of runners? _____

2. Which interval does not have a frequency? _____

Refer to the histogram below to answer the following questions.

3. What information is shown on the frequency axis?
_____

4. What do the intervals show? _____

5. How many employees drive 15 miles or less to work?
_____

6. How many employees drive more than 15 miles to work?
_____

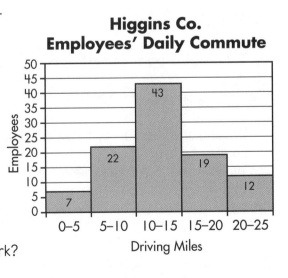

**Higgins Co.
Employees' Daily Commute**

Helping at Home

Encourage your child to research rainfall or snowfall amounts in your area for the past six weeks. Use the data to make a histogram, using appropriate intervals (0– $\frac{1}{8}$ inch, $\frac{1}{8}$ – $\frac{1}{4}$ inch, etc.). What trends in the data does your child notice?

Box Plots

A **box plot** displays data along a number line, using quartiles. **Quartiles** are numbers that divide the data into quarters, or 4 equal parts. The median, or middle quartile, divides the data in half. The lower quartile is the median of the lower half of the data. The upper quartile is the median of the upper half of the data.

Twenty-five percent of the data lies between quartiles. The upper and lower quartiles, enclosing 50% of the data, form the box. The upper extreme (highest value) and lower extreme (lowest value) extend from the box.

To draw a box plot, first arrange the data in order:

12, 13, 14, 14, 15, 16, 17, 18, 19, 19, 21

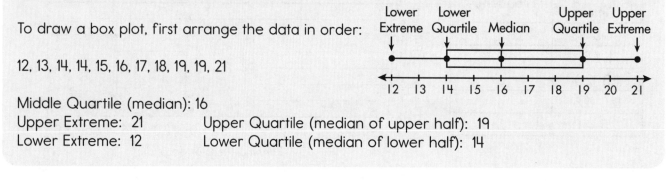

Middle Quartile (median): 16
Upper Extreme: 21   Upper Quartile (median of upper half): 19
Lower Extreme: 12   Lower Quartile (median of lower half): 14

Use the box plot below to answer the following questions.

1. The most miles ridden were _____.

2. The fewest miles ridden were _____.

Miles Ridden in a Bike-a-Thon

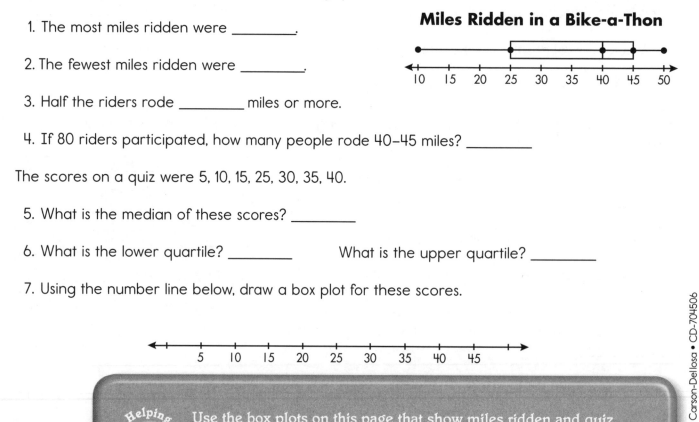

3. Half the riders rode _____ miles or more.

4. If 80 riders participated, how many people rode 40–45 miles? _____

The scores on a quiz were 5, 10, 15, 25, 30, 35, 40.

5. What is the median of these scores? _____

6. What is the lower quartile? _____   What is the upper quartile? _____

7. Using the number line below, draw a box plot for these scores.

Box Plots

A box plot does not show the number of data points. As a result, you cannot use this kind of plot to find the mean or mode. A box plot helps you see at a glance the center, the spread, and the overall range of the data.

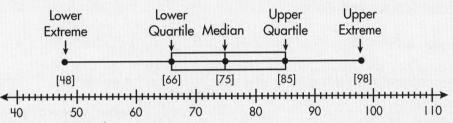

To find the range of the set, subtract the lower extreme from the upper extreme: 98 – 48 = 50. The **interquartile range** is the range of the middle 50% of the data. To find the interquartile range, subtract the lower quartile from the upper quartile: 85 – 66 = 19.

Use the box plots below to answer the questions.

1. The range of wages is _____.

2. The interquartile range is _____.

3. The pay for the top 50% of workers ranges from $ _____ to _____.

Hourly Wages at XYZ Company

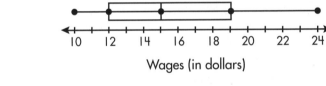

Wages (in dollars)

4. Are wages more spread out for the top 50% or bottom 50% of workers? _____

   How can you tell by looking at the plot? _____

5. The range of passengers is _____.

6. What range of passengers does the middle 50% of flights carry? _____

7. Is it likely that most planes that fly from Airport X can hold at least 300 passengers?

   Explain your answer. _____

Passengers per Flight from Airport X

Passengers (in hundreds)

Using the box plot at the top of this page, ask your child to shade each quartile with a different colored pencil. Help your child understand that even though the quartiles are different lengths, they show equal fourths of the data represented.

Answer Key

Pages 10–11

1. B; 2. D; 3. C; 4. A; 5. C; 6. C; 7. B

Pages 12–13

1. B; 2. C; 3. D; 4. A; 5. C; 6. D; 7. A

Pages 14–15

1. C; 2. B; 3. D; 4. A; 5. B; 6. C; 7. C

Page 17

Answers will vary.

Page 18

1. where food is stored; 2. selfish/stingy;
3. to give; 4. Answers will vary.

Page 19

1. a steep, rugged, rocky cliff; 2. blue;
3. crooked hands, wrinkled sea, crawls, he stands; 4. Answers will vary. 5. The eagle is powerful and swoops down from the sky very quickly.

Page 20

1. Large companies might choose to have their headquarters in Sydney because it is a large city in which to find workers and a major port from which to ship and receive products. 2. 1851; 3. When people came to Sydney looking for gold, they settled there, increasing the population. 4. Answers will vary.

Page 21

1. Large cities develop near water because people and goods can get there easily by ship. 2. The large city of Cairo, Egypt, is a cultural and industrial center. 3. Answers will vary.

Page 22

1. asteroid: any small body that revolves around the Sun in orbit, gaseous: containing gas; 2. about 500 million miles; 3. Jupiter

does not have a solid surface but rather a surface of gaseous clouds. 4. Answers will vary. 5. Jupiter was probably named after the king of the gods because it is the largest planet.

Page 23

1. C; 2. C; 3. A

Page 24

1. Benjamin Franklin was a great colonist who left his mark as a printer, author, inventor, scientist, and statesman. 2. by proving that lightning is a form of electricity; 3. the Declaration of Independence; 4. 6, 3, 4, 2, 5, 1

Page 25

1. where weather occurs; 2. most important; 3. conditions; 4. height above Earth; 5. always

Page 26

1. Francis Scott Key; 2. the American national anthem; 3. 1814; 4. morning; 5. He could see the U.S. flag flying by the light of the rockets and bombs.

Page 27

6. walls of a fort; 7. bravely, proudly;
8. proud; 9. rests, sleeps; 10. D; 11. A;
12. Answers will vary.

Page 28

1. While Australia and New Zealand are often linked, they are individual countries. 2. natural scenery and features; 3. money management; 4. land down under; 5. dairy farming

Page 29

Possible answers: Australia/New Zealand: Australia: continent; dry, flat land; unusual animals; New Zealand: two islands; snowy mountains; volcanic; dairy farming; eat

© Carson-Dellosa • CD-704506

Answer Key

more meat and butter than any other country. Both: "lands down under"; surrounded by water; British settlers; Asian natives.

Australia/United States: Australia: continent; dry, flat land; raise sheep; Southern hemisphere; several marsupials. United States: part of North American continent; varied landscape; raise many types of animals; grain producer; Northern hemisphere; only one marsupial—opossum. Both: farms, bordered by Pacific Ocean; deserts; cities.

Page 30
Answers will vary.

Page 31
Answers will vary.

Page 32
Answers will vary.

Page 33
Answers will vary.

Page 34
Answers will vary.

Page 35
Circled cause and effect words: *so, as a result.* Possible causes and effects: Plates rub against each other./Plates buckle or overlap; Plates buckle or overlap./Surface of Earth shakes or heaves.

Page 36
yes; no; yes; no

Page 37
Answers will vary.

Page 38
Answers will vary.

Page 39
Answers will vary.

Page 40
Circled words in paragraph: *A week later, As soon as, Then;* Answers will vary.

Page 41
Chairman: He is either excited or angry about Morgan being out alone. Kip: He respects the Chairman.

Page 42
1. I, subject; 2. her, possessive; 3. him, object; 4. his, possessive; 5. It, subject; 6. You, subject; 7. me, object; 8. She, subject

Page 43
Matt and Anna, subject; Matt and Anna, subject; Matt and Anna, possessive; Andrew and Stephanie, subject; Matt and Anna, object; Andrew and Stephanie, subject; Matt and Anna, possessive; Andrew and Stephanie, possessive; Andrew and Stephanie, subject; Matt and Anna, possessive; Anna and Stephanie, object; Andrew and Stephanie, possessive; Andrew and Stephanie, possessive

Page 44
1. herself; 2. yourself; 3. themselves; 4. itself; 5. myself; 6. himself; 7. themselves; 8. ourselves

Page 45
2. Has anyone lost his or her wallet lately? 3. Somebody found the wallet under his or her desk. 4. Someone will have to file his or her report. 5. Every dog has its day! 6. I felt Ted had my best interests at heart.

Answer Key

Page 46

1. he; 2. his; 3. its; 4. her; 5. his or her; 6. she; 7. they; 8. her; 9. we; 10. her; 11. its; 12. its; 13. his or her; 14. its; 15. their; 16. his or her

Page 47

1. I love breakfast; I can't imagine skipping it. 2. I scarcely believe I made it all the way down the slope without falling. 3. Samantha doesn't like to wear her coat outside. 4. OK 5. I'm going nowhere until it stops raining. 6. Paul has nothing to contribute to the argument. 7. OK 8. I think nobody can make it to the event early.

Page 48

2. *Horses*; 3. "Brownie"; 4. a convertible; 5. a bracelet; 6. the senator; 7. Karl; 8. Oaties; 9. Samantha; 10. Jones

Page 49

1. enclose numbers; 2. supplementary material; 3. set-off with emphasis; 4. supplementary material; 5. enclose numbers; 6. set-off with emphasis

Page 50

1. C; 2. X; 3. X; 4. C; 5. C; 6. X; 7. C; 8. X; 9. C; 10. C; 11. Answers will vary. 12. Answers will vary.

Page 51

1 discouraged; 2. impatient; 3. assignment; 4. conference; 5. Obviously; 6. practically; 7. additional; 8. recite; 9. column; 10. deceived; 11. courtesy; 12. invisible; 13. conversation; 14. comparison; 15. Popularity; 16. achievement; 17. condemned

Page 52

1. combined adverb and verb; 2. combined subjects; 3. combined adjective and noun; 4. combined verbs; 5. subordinate conjunction

Page 53

2. self, self having a mind, self-acting or self-motivating; 3. to do, to do across, to carry on or conduct a settlement; 4. a hundred, a hundred meters, one-hundredth of a meter; 5. water, water sailor, an underwater explorer

Page 54

2. carry, carry again, to carry and repeat, as in a message; 3. to come, to come between, to come between; 4. lead, lead in, to lead by persuasion; 5. to look, to look backward, to look back on past events; 6. carry, carry again, to hand over for consideration; 7. to hold, to hold again, to keep possession of

Page 55

1. chronological; 2. homophones; 3. biography; 4. tricycle; 5. manual; 6. thermos; 7. Cyclops; 1. recycling; 2. chronicles; 3. thermostat

Page 56

1. annual; 2. auditorium; 3. liberty; 4. millipede; 5. aquamarine; 6. maritime; 7. pedal

Page 57

1. cricket; 2. contain; 3. rub; 4. dragonfly; 5. divide; 6. mosquito; 7. find; 8. soar; 1. Possible answer: Try not to squash the flowers when you are playing ball in the yard. 2. sincere; 3. reflection/regal; 4. five

Page 58

1. leaves, tiny hands; 2. golf balls, round eggs; 3. house, icebox; 4. dog's tail, flag; 5. seashells, tiny treasures; 6. Davis, warrior; 7. lights of the city, constellation

Page 59

1. gaping mouth; 2. sprang to life; 3. blinked; 4. struggled, hoping; 5. coughed and

Answer Key

sputtered as if it wanted to breathe;
6. eyeing; 7. smile; 8. sipped; 1. Answers will
vary. 2. Answers will vary. 3. Answers will vary.

Page 60

1. Increase; 2. copy; 3. foot; 4. second;
5. Often; 6. March; 7. student; 8. carrots;
9. food; 10. cleaning; 11. twenty-four;
12. instrument; 13. sweet

Page 61

1. Detroit; 2. sport; 3. lead; 4. princess; 5. web;
6. seedling; 7. bracelet; 8. patients; 1. e; 2. a; 3.
f; 4. e; 5. d; 6. c; 7. b

Page 62

job; mature; respond; remainder; proud;
conversational; abundantly; relaxed; hut;
curious; swift; scamp

Page 63

Possible answers: bountiful; disagreement;
corrected; talked; wrote; suddenly; serious;
took; refused; messy

Page 68

1. true, false, true; 2. false, true, false; 3. false,
true, true; 4. true, false, false; 5. C

Page 69

1. $3.95; 2. $1.25; 3. $15.25; 4. 130 British pounds

Page 70

1. 200 lb.; 2. 64; 3. 20; 4. 80 mi.; 5. 72; 6. 27; 7.
4 cm

Page 71

1. $200

Boxes (x values)	Dollars (y values)
2	40
4	80
6	120
8	160

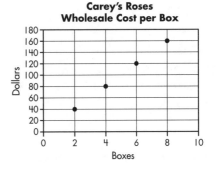

Carey's Roses
Wholesale Cost per Box

Page 72

1. Jack consistently used less gas than Bob
did over the same distance.

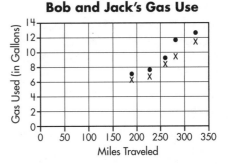

Bob and Jack's Gas Use

2. Grade increases as study hours increase.

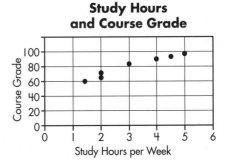

Study Hours
and Course Grade

Page 73

1. $\frac{1}{5}$, 37.5, $1\frac{1}{5}$; 2. 262.5, $\frac{41}{50}$, $\frac{57}{400}$; 3. $1\frac{16}{25}$, 35, 16; 4.
95, $2\frac{12}{25}$, 330; 5. 0.0575, 12.5, 0.58; 6. 115, 0.09,
3.5; 7. 2.25, 0.5, 0.99; 8. 80, 382, 0.5225

Page 74

1. $5\frac{1}{5}$, 76; 2. $9\frac{3}{5}$, 7; 3. 18, $7\frac{1}{2}$; 4. $1\frac{24}{25}$, $3\frac{4}{5}$; 5. 8,
$6\frac{3}{4}$; 6. 64, 15; 7. $31\frac{1}{2}$, $8\frac{1}{10}$; 8. $3\frac{17}{25}$, $14\frac{2}{5}$; 9. 54,

Answer Key

$21\frac{1}{2}$; 10. $4\frac{4}{5}$, $5\frac{2}{5}$; 11. 36, 19; 12. $10\frac{1}{2}$, $\frac{3}{4}$

Page 75

1. 20.48, 10.4; 2. 2.225, 4.62; 3. 6.96, 20; 4. 6.132, 42.14; 5. 2.048, 3.19; 6. 42, 4.5; 7. 5.88, 38; 8. 9, 31.24; 9. 5.746, 64; 10. 7.84, 27.9

Page 76

1. $48.65; 2. $194.60; 3. 18; 4. 480; 5. $90; 6. 375

Page 77

1. 84 in., 6 ft., 45 ft.; 2. 3 yd., 21,120 ft., 7,040 yd.; 3. 9 ft., 10 ft., 14 yd.; 4. 55 in., 81 in., $2\frac{1}{2}$ ft.; 5. 3 mi., 18 ft., 216 in.; 6. 23 ft., 276 in., 8 yd.; 7. 141 in., 11,060 ft., 10 yd.; 8. 300 in., 12 ft., 4 yd.; 9. 8,800 yd., $1\frac{1}{2}$ ft., 36 ft.; 10. 432 in., $\frac{1}{2}$ mi., 188 in.

Page 78

1. 4,000 g, 0.004 kg, 4,000 mg; 2. 0.073 g, 3,660 g, 0.03 g; 3. 2,600 g, 0.265 kg, 40,000 mg; 4. 0.9 kg, 720 mg, 0.0008 kg; 5. 0.492 kg, 0.006 kg, 6,000 mg; 6. 86.4 kg, 1,200 g, 0.004 g; 7. 1.6 kg; 8. 440 kg; 9. 11.39 kg

Page 79

1. $\frac{5}{6}$, $\frac{9}{16}$, $\frac{5}{6}$, $1\frac{1}{15}$; 2. $\frac{4}{7}$, $1\frac{1}{15}$, $2\frac{2}{9}$, $\frac{5}{6}$; 3. $2\frac{5}{8}$, $1\frac{1}{6}$, $\frac{1}{2}$, $2\frac{1}{2}$; 4. $\frac{9}{10}$, $1\frac{1}{27}$, $\frac{4}{5}$, $\frac{6}{7}$

Page 80

1. $\frac{3}{4}$, $\frac{1}{2}$, $2\frac{2}{7}$, $\frac{7}{15}$; 2. $3\frac{6}{7}$, $2\frac{1}{72}$, $\frac{13}{18}$, $\frac{12}{25}$; 3. $2\frac{2}{5}$, $\frac{1}{2}$, $1\frac{1}{3}$, $\frac{17}{24}$; 4. $\frac{9}{10}$, $1\frac{23}{57}$, $\frac{3}{13}$, $5\frac{2}{5}$

Page 81

1. $3\frac{1}{16}$; 2. 8; 3. $\frac{7}{27}$; 4. $1\frac{1}{3}$; 5. 5; 6. $2\frac{2}{5}$

Page 82

1. 5r4, 2r14, 4, 4r2, 2r14; 2. 2r2, 7, 27r1, 32, 29r14; 3. 30r5, 13r23, 19r25, 26r17, 18

Page 83

1. 110r25, 312, 115r21, 179r2, 110; 2. 154r20, 113, 270r2, 523, 225; 3. 1467r1, 725, 828r40, 886, 569

Page 84

1. 11.7, 1.61, 4.23, 9.81, 20.44; 2. 2.315, 40.21, 44.339, 10.52, 6.35; 3. 10.45, 70.79, 134.99, 33.5, 22.3; 4. 8.1, 77.16, 46.344, 101.1, 4; 5. 15.22, 590.13, 204.11, 28.205, 16.884; 6. 0.771, 12.596, 94.211, 8.142, 102.5

Page 85

1. 0.5, 0.8, 1.9, 0.69, 1.5; 2. 7.04, 0.163, 0.335, 1.3, 2.8; 3. 16.3, 0.37, 0.33, 2.567, 7.11; 4. 4.218, 14.4, 24.232, 5.9, 7.76; 5. 16.8, 9.145, 26.16, 41.7, 95.3; 6. 1.86, 1.462, 2.69, 1.3, 4.9

Page 86

1. 5.6, 0.04, 0.0975, 13.44, 17.5; 2. 0.0918, 0.0486, 28.105, 2.1087, 275.04; 3. 19.8468, 206.703, 303.986, 20.4102, 563.85; 4. 95.934, 58.734, 15.036, 2.2382, 0.6724

Page 87

1. 0.21, 56, 3, 51; 2. 36, 3.5, 4200, 24.58; 3. 0.09, 452, 500, 1.6

Page 88

1. Factors: 1, 2, 4, 8 and 1, 2, 3, 4, 6, 12. Common factors: 1, 2, 4. Greatest common factor: 4. 2. Factors: 1, 2, 3, 6 and 1, 2, 3, 6, 9, 18. Common factors: 1, 2, 3, 6. Greatest common factor: 6. 3. Factors: 1, 2, 3, 4, 6, 8, 12, 24 and 3, 5, 15. Common factors: 1, 3. Greatest common factor: 3. 4. Factors: 1, 2, 4 and 1, 2, 3, 6. Common factors: 1, 2. Greatest common factor: 2. 5. Factors: 1, 5 and 1, 2, 3, 4, 6, 12. Common factors: 1. Greatest common factor: 1. 6. Factors: 1, 2, 4, 8, 16 and 1, 2, 3, 4, 6, 12. Common factors: 1, 2, 4. Greatest common factor: 4.

© Carson-Dellosa • CD-704506

Answer Key

Page 89

1. $\frac{5}{30}$ and $\frac{12}{30}$, $\frac{9}{24}$ and $\frac{8}{24}$; 2. $\frac{21}{28}$ and $\frac{4}{28}$, $\frac{2}{12}$ and $\frac{9}{12}$; 3. $\frac{4}{8}$ and $\frac{5}{8}$, $\frac{5}{20}$ and $\frac{6}{20}$; 4. $\frac{9}{45}$ and $\frac{20}{45}$, $\frac{8}{20}$ and $\frac{5}{20}$

Page 90

1. –2, –7, 1; 2. 6, 3, –5; 3. 2 < 7, –1 > –4, 5 > 0; 4. –4 < 1, 0 > –8, –8 > –10; 5. 7 > –7, –2 < 0, 4 < 6; 6. –5, –3, 0 and –8, 2, 8; 7. –7, –3, 0, 5 and –2, –1, 2, 4

Page 91

1. 23; 2. 36°; 3. –16; 4. 4299 ft.; 5. 1229; 6. 14551

Page 92

1. D, A; 2. E, C; 3. F, B; 4. (–4, 3), (–4, –2); 5. (–2, –3), (1, –3); 6. (2, 1), (2, 3); 7.–9.

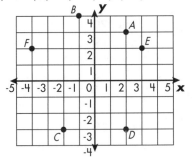

Page 93

1. 8, 5, –2, 5; 2. –8, 3, –10, 10; 3. 3, –9, –1, –23; 4. –15, 1, –5, –11; 5. –16, –11, 2, –5; 6. –15, –10, 43, –15; 7. –9, 1, –1, 0; 8. 0, –11, –4, –1

Page 94

1. multiply, multiply, add; 2. subtract, divide, divide; 3. add, subtract, add; 4. 10, 23; 5. 8, 8; 6. 9, 1; 7. 8, 20; 8. 10, 2; 9. 8, 8; 10. 40, 40

Page 95

1. 5^3, 3^6, b^4; 2. 23^1, n^5, 12^2; 3. 27, 121, 1; 4. 625, 100000, 55; 5. 17, 36, 64, 2; 6. 87, 64, 22, 1

Page 96

1. expression, equation, expression; 2. 3, x and 4, y; 3. n + 5, 8 – x; 4. x + 7, n × 11; 5. 6n =18, 70 – n =29; 6. $\frac{8}{n}$ = 2, 7 × 12 = 84; 7. Six decreased by a number is equal to three. 8. The product of five and thirteen is equal to sixty-five.

Page 97

1. x – 5; 2. 3(y + 12); 3. 10 + $\frac{c}{3}$; 4. 2 + 6x; 5. $\frac{2}{3}$y – 11; 6. 2(c – 4); 7. 9x – 7; 8. 6n + 7n; 9. n + 2n; 10. $\frac{1}{4}$x +11

Page 98

1. –2; 2. 8; 3. 40; 4. 26; 5. –3; 6. 42; 7. –12; 8. 17; 9. 4; 10. –13; 11. –88; 12. 22; 13. –90; 14. 486; 15. –192; 16. –6

Page 99

1. multiply, add; 2. add, multiply; 3. (4 × 6) + (4 × 2), 2 × (5 + 4); 4. 5 × (1 + 6), (4 × 2) + (4 × 6); 5. 5, 2; 6. 6, 5; 7. 16, 16; 8. 21, 25

Page 100

1. –7a – 7b; 2. xy – 4x; 3. $\frac{2}{3}$ c + 8; 4. –4t + –48; 5. 2xy – 16y; 6. 6a – 24b; 7. 6xy – 12x; 8. 56z – 35x; 9. 50y – 30yz; 10. 21x – 24xy; 1. 15y – 2; 2. 4a – 1; 3. 15a – 2b; 4. 11xy; 5. 16 – 15m; 6. 4a – 1; 7. 26x – 25y; 8. 15c – 8ab – 10; 9. 44ab + –6a + –14b; 10. 33x – 16xy

Page 101

1. addition, subtraction; 2. subtraction, addition; 3. 6, 4, 17; 4. 11, 12, 0; 5. 12, 10, 0; 6. 3, 21, 9; 7. 0, 20, 4; 8. 8, 30, 15, 10; 9. x + $6 = $20, x = $14; 10. g + 12 = 27, g = 15

Page 102

1. divide, multiply; 2. multiply, divide; 3. 3, 25, 12; 4. 9, 1, 8; 5. 2, 16, 5; 6. 3, 2 $\frac{1}{2}$, 10; 7. $\frac{1}{4}$, 20, 81; 8. 2, 40, 3; 9. 36, 6, 10; 10. 40, 16, 1

Page 103

1. >, >, <; 2. >, <, <; 3. =, <, =; 4. <, >, >

Answer Key

Page 104

1. $x > 3$, $t < 15$, $m > 6$; 2. $y \leq 10$, $r \geq -4$, $n \leq 8$; 3. $p < -6$, $z < 20$, $w \geq -16$; 4. $x \geq 14$, $p \leq 31$, $y \leq 24$; 5. $n + \$16.50 \leq \$25$, $n \leq \$8.50$

Page 105

1. $y < 3$, $k > 42$, $n \geq 3$; 2. $h < -4$, $m > -20$, $c \geq -12$; 3. $p < 2$, $n \geq 27$, $a > 10$; 4. $n < -1$, $b \leq -6$, $x > 16$; 5. $\$6.25\,n \leq \$26$, $n \leq 4.16$

Page 106

1. 54 yd.², 72 cm², 64 in.²; 2. 15 km, 10 m, 32 ft.

Page 107

1. 40 ft.², 33 cm², 27.5 in.²; 2. 32 m², 72 yd.², 405 cm²

Page 108

1. 121.5 in.², 20 km², 64 ft.²; 2. 108 cm², 1250 m², 13.5 in.²

Page 109

1. 100 cm², 17.5 km², 20 in.²; 2. 725 m², 77 in.², 81 cm²

Page 110

1. 576 cu. cm, 1,728 cu. cm, 2,112 cu. m; 2. 144 cu. mm, 1,620 cu. mm, 3,600 cu. cm; 3. 1,280 cu. mm, 12,000 cu. cm, 7,800 cu. mm

Page 111

1. B, 14 cm²; 2. A, 16 cm²; 3. C, 22 cm²;

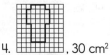

4. , 30 cm²

Page 113

Answers will vary, but should answer the original question and include a comparison between males and females. Example: Dogs are the most popular pet overall, but males prefer dogs more strongly than females do.

Page 114

1. $35\frac{3}{5}$, 35, 43, 18 and 14, 12, 12, 15; 2. 68, 71, 79, 27 and 51, 49, 37, 49

Page 115

1. 81, 84, 88, 93, 97, mean: 88.6, median: 88, mode: none, range: 16; 2. 83, 84, 84, 85, 86, mean: 84.4, median: 84, mode: 84, range: 3; 3. 85, 88, 90, 92, 92, mean: 89.4, median: 90, mode: 92, range: 7; 4. Kara, because her scores had the smallest range.

Page 116

1. $9.41, $9.75; 2. $9.50, $8.25; 3. $9.50 and $10, $8; 4. Sam's Pet World pays better. The $20 wage in the set for Beth's Pets is an outlier that increases the mean above Sam's. However, the higher median and mode show that most of Sam's employees are paid better.

Page 117

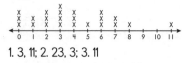

1. 3, 11; 2. 23, 3; 3. 11

Page 118

1. 56 and 57; 2. 25; 3. 26; 4. 56.5; 5. Possible answer: from 54 through 60 transactions, because most clerks have been performing within this cluster of transactions; 6. Possible answer: above 65 transactions, because a number beyond 65 would be an outlier, indicating an exceptionally high number of transactions

Page 119

1. 11.5–12.0; 2. 11–11.5; 3. number of employees; 4. driving miles; 5. 72; 6. 31

Page 120

1. 50; 2. 10; 3. 40; 4. 20; 5. 25; 6. 10, 35; 7.

Page 121

1. 14; 2. 7; 3. $15, $24; 4. top 50%, the distance from the median to the upper extreme appears greater than to the lower extreme; 5. 300; 6. 150; 7. yes, because 50% of flights carry 300 or more passengers, and planes this size could be responsible for some of the flights carrying fewer than 300